Home Winemaking

Step by Step

Home
Winemaking

Step by Step

A Guide to
Fermenting Wine Grapes

THIRD EDITION

REVISED

———

JON IVERSON

Stonemark Publishing Co.

Cover design: Patricia Broersma
Interior illustrations: Sarah Cribb
Book design: Wellstone Press

ISBN 0-9657936-3-X

Third edition, revised

Library of Congress Catalog Card No.
00-90581

Printed in the United States of America

STONEMARK PUBLISHING COMPANY
P.O. Box 687
Medford, OR 97501

Contents

Home Winemaking

Step by Step

QUANTITIES

Grapes —As a rule of thumb, 100 pounds of grapes will yield a gross total of 6 gallons (U.S.) of juice and pulp and a net of 5 gallons of finished wine after settling and racking losses. This will vary depending on the relative water content of the grapes, how hard they are pressed, whether you settle out the pulp and ferment only the clear juice, and whether you use pectic enzyme, which will release more of the liquid but also create more pulp. Red grapes will usually yield slightly more because they are fermented on the skins and more liquid is released before pressing.

Sugar —If the juice needs to be sweetened, $1^1/_2$ ounces of table sugar per U.S. gallon will raise the Brix by 1°.

Acid —One level teaspoon per U.S. gallon of tartaric acid, malic acid or acid blend will raise the total acidity of a wine or must by approximately .12%. See *Appendix A* for testing total acidity and page 87 for further details on these acids.

Potassium metabisulfite — $^1/_4$ tsp per 5 U.S. gallons = 50 parts per million (ppm). Use 50 ppm at crushing (optional), 50 ppm at first racking, and 50 ppm when bottling. Always dissolve it in a bit of water first and stir it in very well. See page 219 for use of a 10% stock sulfite solution.

INTRODUCTION

he first few chapters of this book will lead you successfully through the crushing, pressing, fermenting and clarifying steps of making white wines, as well as the bottling. White wines are a good place to start in understanding the art of fermenting wines, as it forces you to appreciate the pernicious effects of air. Minimize air contact, limit the use of meta, don't over-oak, and you will actually find it easier to make a good white wine than red.

There are a number of reasons white wines are easier than reds. The small amount of unfermented or "residual" sugar present in white wines tends to conceal flaws in the grapes and makes fruit quality less critical. In contrast, red wines are normally bottled "bone dry;" i.e., with no residual sugar. As a result, high acidity, low pH or flaws in the fruit quality are more easily detected in a finished red wine. The quality of the fruit has to be higher to make an outstanding red wine.

White wines are also easier in that they are fermented cooler and are not as prone to spoilage problems during fermentation. Red grapes are normally fermented at higher temperatures in order to extract maximum flavor from the skins. The higher fermentation temperature increases the risk of spoilage and unwanted side reactions involving volatile acids.

In my experience, it has been easier to find quality white grapes than red, and at less cost. This will, of course, depend on the supply and demand situation in your area. The quality of white grapes seems to suffer less from the common practice of over-cropping than does the quality of red grapes. Since most white grapes ripen earlier than reds, the white grape crop is less often affected by early rains and frosts. If you have tried white wines in the past and had only marginal success, don't give up! Follow the basic procedures discussed in chapter 1 through chapter 5, and you'll be well rewarded.

If, as has been said, "the first duty of a wine is to be red," it follows that the first duty of a winemaker is to make red wines! The discussion of fermentation of red wines in chapter 6, along with fermenting variations for red wines in chapter 11 and malolactic fermentation in chapter 12, covers all the techniques that can readily be used by a home winemaker.

You can make excellent red wines without going beyond chapter 6, and I highly recommend that beginning winemakers do just that—stick to the basics in chapter 6 and ignore the more advanced procedures discussed in chapter 11 and chapter 12. If you are a beginning winemaker intent on making red wines, be sure to read the earlier chapters on white winemaking. Some of the procedures are treated in greater detail there.

Glossaries of equipment and supplies are included at the end of several chapters. These are intended to be a reference source as needed. Note that not every term used in this book is fully defined. Just remember that "racking" means siphoning from one container to another and that potassium metabisulfite, meta, sulfite and SO_2 are synonyms, and you will get by very well!

Chapter One

GETTING STARTED

he art of making wine has evolved a great deal in the last twenty or thirty years, and the progress shows no sign of slowing. Never in the history of mankind has it been possible to make wine of such high quality from a given batch of grapes. Great strides have been made both in growing premium grapes and in extracting the maximum from the fruit. The advances benefit the home winemaker as well as the commercial. With the expanded array of equipment and supplies now available, the home winemaker can routinely make wines that exceed the quality of ordinary commercial wines. In fact, if you ferment the same grapes from the same vineyard, your wine should be better than the winery's! The home winemaker has an edge in working with small quantities and being able to clarify without having to pump and filter. The quality of your wine will be limited only by the quality of the grapes you crush and ferment.

Good grapes

This subject is as impossible to discuss as it is important! If omitted, the reader could legitimately ask why it was not included. So here goes. The reason grape quality is so important is that good grapes are the basis for any good wine. The better the grapes, the better the wine will be. Any honest vintner will admit that when the grapes come in good, the wine literally makes itself. It ferments without problems, clarifies readily and needs no adjustments before or after fermentation. On the other hand, if the grapes are poor, the best vintner in the world will not be able to make a great wine out of them.

There is no simple answer to the very elusive question of what makes a good grape. Grapes cannot be judged by appearance because sunburned grapes with broken skins are likely to make a better wine than perfect looking clusters. Nor do acid, sugar and pH readings tell the whole story because growing conditions differ from year to year. Here are some general considerations, laden with my biases.

Yield. Tons per acre is one of the biggest factors in determining quality. The growers like to believe that a heavy crop does not affect quality, as long as it ripens fully. Vintners believe that a light crop is inherently better than a heavy crop. Historically, the best wines have come in years when Mother Nature imposed a low yield per acre. It is also significant that wineries growing their own grapes and making premium wines will intentionally drop fruit during the growing season.

On the other hand, the growers correctly point out that with the right variety and right clone on the right site, very heavy yields of

Doug and Marlene Moorhead of Moorhead Vineyards, North East, Pennsylvania, examining their viognier vines.

Peter Brehm kneeling by his Chardonnay vines at White Salmon Vineyard, in Underwood, Washington

very high quality grapes can be grown, with almost no loss in quality. Obviously, there is no definitive answer to the controversial subject of yield.

Variety. Some varieties suffer more from over-cropping than others, Chardonnay and Pinot Noir being two such that come to mind. Cabernet Sauvignon and Merlot are less affected and some of the other white varieties are even less affected. However, over-cropping always takes a toll. This means that if the yield looks to be 30% or 40% below normal, it should be a good year and you should start in early July trying to line up a source of grapes. It may take more effort because the wineries will compete harder for the reduced crop.

Irrigation. This is another subject on which the interest of the growers differs from the wineries. There is an inherent conflict of interest between the two in that the grower wants to maximize the yield and the winery wants the maximum quality. The problem is that few wineries are willing to pay the grower twice as much per pound for dropping half the grapes. So unless the grower has a contract with a winery, he will be inclined to water generously to increase the yield; but this dilutes quality. The plumper the grape, the higher the ratio of juice-to-skin. The best wines are thought to come from small berries because there is more skin surface relative to the volume of liquid. Although the best grapes probably come from grapes that have been dry-farmed, the effect of watering can be greatly reduced by stopping all irrigation during the six weeks prior to harvest. This allows the berries to shrink as harvest approaches. Since dry farming is a rarity in most areas, the next best choice would be drip irrigation. A vineyard with state-of-the-art drip irrigation most likely has a knowledgeable grower, and the grapes will have suffered less from fungal and pest problems.

Specific vineyards. Due to a combination of factors, some vineyards will produce superior fruit year in and year out. The depth and composition of the soil are big factors. All else being equal, vines in shallow and poor soil are thought to produce better grapes than vines in deep, fertile soil. The availability of water is similarly related—grapes from a vineyard with abundant subterranean water will probably not measure up to those from a nearby vineyard with little underground water. Talk to vintners in your area to find out which vineyards and growers have the best reputation. I have found vintners to be as approachable and friendly as they are dedicated to their art! Everything else being equal, I would favor the vineyard that sells to respected wineries.

Finding good grapes

The first, and always the most important, order of business is lining up a source of good grapes. The earlier in the year you establish contact with possible sources, the more likely you will be rewarded with quality grapes in the fall. If you

Donna Lailey checking the set on her Cabernet Franc vines at her Niagara-on-the-Lake Vineyard, Ontario.

live in a grape growing region, start calling vineyards in early summer. By late June, they will know the extent of the fruit set and will be more willing to make a commitment. Some will want part of the money up front, which is a reasonable request if they are expected to reserve fruit for you. Some growers cater to home winemakers because they get top dollar for their fruit. And it's all cash to the grower, which isn't always the case when they sell to commercial wineries. Once you find a good source, stay with it year after year. A continuing relationship is your best chance of getting grapes in years of scarcity and high demand.

Some wine supply stores make arrangements to buy grapes from growers and resell to amateurs. This convenience is worth the extra cost, and there is comfort in knowing that the grapes were likely picked at their peak. In the case of white grapes, some stores will even crush, press and sell you the juice, or "must" as it is called in winemaking parlance. This should have particular appeal to someone who plans to process small batches of grapes or who is uncertain about winemaking as a hobby. It saves the expense of purchasing or renting equipment.

The natural tendency is to ferment small quantities of several varieties. Although it is interesting to have several varieties, you will soon discover that it takes little more effort to process two or three hundred pounds of a given variety than one hundred pounds. A larger quantity also gives you the ability to ferment 5 gallons in one manner and 5 gallons in another. And starting with more, you are more likely to have a little left in two or three years, when the wine is reaching its peak! It is perfectly acceptable to ferment small batches; it's just that if you become serious about home winemaking, you will most likely lean toward larger quantities of fewer varieties.

Alternatives to fresh grapes

Most serious winemakers are probably reading the next section already. The rest of you, take note! There are some excellent juices available in forms which are not only easier to work with than fresh grapes but which generally eliminate the need for a crusher, crusher-stemmer or press. The reason I include this section is that many home winemakers do not live in wine growing regions. Even those who do will discover that locating a source of grapes is only the beginning. When the grapes ripen, there is a fairly short window of opportunity during which the grapes are at their peak and should be picked. This means that you might have to drop everything and go get them on short notice, often during the middle of the week. This very sizeable investment of time and planning can be circumvented by using frozen must, aseptic juice or concentrate kits rather than fresh grapes. If high quality grapes were used, some of these alternatives would probably make a better wine than fresh grapes of low quality. So, don't rule these alternatives out.

If fresh grapes were not available to me and I was intent on making high quality wine, my first choice would be frozen musts. These are grapes that have been crushed, possibly sulfited and then frozen. The buckets start thawing during shipment by UPS and can be fermented shortly after arrival. White grapes have been crushed and pressed. You ferment pure juice, so neither crusher nor press will be needed. Just follow the basic procedure for fermenting white wines as outlined in chapter 2.

Red varieties arrive crushed and de-stemmed, so you will not need a crusher-stemmer. Just add a yeast starter and ferment in a primary fermenter for a few days, punching down as discussed in chapter 6. A 5-gallon bucket of frozen must will yield about 3 gallons of finished wine. Five gallons can easily be pressed in a nylon mesh bag, but a press is a necessity with large volumes. A nylon bag requires a little more effort than a press, but you will get almost as much wine. And it is quicker to use rubber gloves and a nylon bag because there is no set up or clean up.

There is virtually no loss of quality as a result of freezing a must. Frozen musts are generally available on a first-come basis, so it tends to be a seasonal proposition. It will pay to get your name on the list early.

If frozen musts were not available, "aseptic" juices would be my next choice. If the same grapes were being processed, the quality should be only slightly lower than a frozen must. Rather than being frozen, the juice is flash pasteurized, sulfited, bagged and boxed. The juice has not been reduced in volume by boiling, as have the concentrates discussed below. Neither press nor crusher-stemmer is needed, even in the case of red grapes, as the skins have been processed and added back for pigment and complexity. After pasteurization, a controlled amount of sulfite is added and the juice is bagged and boxed. The home winemaker simply transfers the juice to a primary fermenter and ferments with no ado. No grapes to crush or de-stem, no punching down and no equipment to clean up! The wine can be fermented in a primary fermenter for 3 or 4 days and then transferred to carboys, topped with an air lock and allowed to ferment to dryness. However, I prefer to ferment in carboys two-thirds full from start to finish. Follow the basic procedure in chapter 2. Bottle a red wine bone dry; sweeten a white wine slightly before bottling, as discussed in chapters 3 and 4.

"Concentrate kits" are relatively new and superior in quality to the canned concentrates that have been around for decades. They are referenced as "kits" because they come packaged with all the essentials, such as sulfite, potassium sorbate, bentonite, isinglass or gelatin, oak flavoring, finishing agent and the like. Like aseptic juices, concentrate kits come bagged and boxed. However, after being flash pasteurized, they are reduced in volume by boiling at low temperatures in a vacuum. They are not reduced as much as the traditional canned concentrates, so the quality remains higher. Six gallons of juice might be reduced to 4 gallons or 3 gallons. The winemaker adds water back to bring the volume back up to 6 gallons and ferments according to directions. The shipping and storage costs are less, so the overall cost is less.

The traditional canned concentrates have been reduced the most in volume. The instructions typically call for adding 3 gallons of water to 1 gallon of concentrate. They have been processed longer than concentrate kits and probably subjected to more heat. Fruit quality being equal, the quality of canned concentrates should be lower.

Although grapes of very high quality are sold as frozen musts, the very finest grapes will not be found in concentrates. Neither the processor nor the home winemaker could afford it. Grape quality is still critical, and some processors will use better grapes than others. In addition to grape quality, the sophistication of the industrial process used to make the concentrate is important to the ultimate quality. The better the vacuum, the lower the temperature at which the liquid will boil, and the less of the essence of the grape that is lost. Although all processors will trap the phenols and organic compounds that are boiled off and add them back before canning, a lower temperature and more gentle processing

Joe Nardone, Rochester, New York, checking the Brix in primary fermenters handed down from his father.

will retain more of these subtle organic compounds. Don't hesitate to ask questions about the processing method before deciding on a concentrate. (See chapter 15 and appendix G for more on fermenting aseptic juices and concentrate kits.)

Equipment and supplies

You will also need to decide on equipment and supplies. Some items are essential at the outset, while certain others can wait until bottling or until next year. Some pieces can be improvised. Some are luxury items that you will never buy unless winemaking becomes a serious hobby.

The first stop should be your local winemaking supply store. If the Yellow Pages for your area have no listings under "beer and winemaking supplies," try a large metropolitan area. Call and ask for a catalog. Many wine supply shops have catalogs and are happy to ship. Shopping by mail is easy with toll-free numbers, FAX machines and UPS delivery.

If you will be fermenting aseptic juice or concentrates, you will not have to worry about the main pieces of winemaking equipment — the crusher and the press. If you plan to process only small quantities of fresh grapes to begin with, try renting a crusher and press, as the cash outlay to purchase is substantial. If you find yourself totally without access to equipment, small quantities of grapes can be crushed with a 4X4 post or even with your foot and pressed by hand in a nylon mesh bag! (Be careful, however, not to crack the seeds if crushing with a hard object, as they contain large amounts of highly-astringent tannin). But if you have much more than 100 pounds to process, try your best to borrow, rent or purchase a crusher and press.

Once you've made the decision to invest in equipment, try placing an ad in the "Miscellaneous Wanted" section of your newspaper classified ads. There are always retired home winemakers willing to part with used carboys, crushers and presses for much less than replacement cost. Most equipment lasts indefinitely, and used equipment is usually as functional as new. And whether you are considering new or used equipment, the initial investment can be kept even lower and more fun can be had if several people go in together and pool their resources!

Equipment Glossary

The array of equipment available to the home winemaker has improved steadily over the years. It would take a tidy sum to buy everything at once, but you do not need everything at the outset in order to make quality wines. Here's a list of standard equipment and supplies. Note that plastic, polyethylene and polypropylene materials for pails, hoses and other materials that come in contact with the wine should be of food grade quality. This is indicated by a "USDA" or "HDPE" imprint. (Parentheses indicate that an item is not essential).

Notebook. Get a substantial notebook to keep notes. Some winemakers hang a tag around the neck of each carboy for immediately recording what was done and transfer the data to the permanent notebook later. I settled on a 3-ring binder with heavy mylar-reinforced notebook paper. Whatever technique you use, good notes are important.

CRUSHER. The threshold question in deciding on a crusher is whether you are primarily interested in white wines or red wines. For processing white grapes, a simple crusher with two meshed rollers is preferable to a crusher-stemmer.

CRUSHER  —— grape skins, stems, and juice

White grapes should be left on the stems for pressing, as the stems stabilize the mass inside the press and allow the juice to flow more freely.

A crusher-stemmer, however, is better for processing red grapes because the stems have to be separated before fermentation, and it does this automatically.

CRUSHER-STEMMER

stems

—— grape skins and juice

With a small quantity of red grapes, the stems can be fished out with a homemade rake, such as long stainless steel screws in a board, or even by hand. But with larger quantities, a crusher-stemmer is nearly indispensable. Unfortunately, crusher-stemmers are considerably more expensive than plain crushers, even if not motorized.

Whether you are looking at a plain crusher or a crusher-stemmer, consider getting a stainless steel hopper. It's worth the extra cost in the long run. Washing and maintenance will be less critical, and you will not have to worry about contamination with trace amounts of metals.

PRESS. A good press is the other basic piece of winemaking equipment. The screw-type, vertical basket press of Italian origin has been around forever and works well. The larger the press, the less efficient it is at extracting the juice, due to the diminishing surface-to-volume ratio as the size increases. If you plan to do mostly white wines and want to extract as much juice as possible, a smaller size might be preferable. The No. 30 size — about 7.5 gallons — will press 100 pounds of white grapes before it has to be split apart to dispose of the cake of skins and stems, or "pomace." Double that poundage if you are pressing red grapes after fermentation on the skins. Bladder presses are better than the traditional press but considerably more expensive. And the bladders oxidize with age and have to be replaced, which is an extra expense.

Consider building or buying a stand to mount your press on. Not only will the press be more stable, but the added height will allow the use of larger containers to catch the juice as you press.

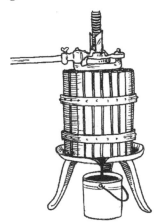

PRIMARY FERMENTERS. At least one primary fermenter will be needed. Red wines are initially fermented in an open container, preferably one with a lid or cover. Although white wines are best fermented in carboys, a primary fermenter will be needed anyway to hold the grapes and juice as they are crushed. And they are convenient for transporting grapes. So at least one primary fermenter, such as a Rubbermaid Brute®, should be on the shopping list. Or, you could get 55-gallon poly barrels which have been used to transport fruit juices (see photo next page). Fruit juice brokers and cold storage warehouses often have them available for $10 or so, and they will accommodate up to 400 pounds of red grapes. Be sure you know what they contained before as the material will pick up a taint.

Fifteen-gallon beer kegs are probably the most commonly used primary fermenter as they are probably the least expensive, gallon for gallon.

A line of poly tanks manufactured by Graf and imported from Italy is available from some sources (see photo next page). They come in 60, 100 and 200 liter sizes and are ideal because they have a wide, screw-top lid with an air lock, plus a plug for draining. These tanks can be used as a primary fermenter for either white wines or red wines, with or without the skins. The wide mouth allows crushed grapes and juice to be poured in, making them an excellent choice for extended maceration or carbonic maceration of red grapes. Needless to say, the price is several times that of a plain "garbage can" of food quality.

Fifty-five gallon poly barrel

If cost is not a factor, consider a 304 stainless steel vat with a floating lid. These containers are available in various sizes starting at 20 gallons. The lid has an inflatable tube around it, similar to a bicycle inner tube, which can be pumped up to make the fermenter airtight. Although a container of this type could be used to ferment almost any wine, it is especially desirable for extended maceration of red grapes after fermentation is complete.

PAILS. Two or three plastic pails will be needed to catch the juice as it flows out of the press, to dip crushed grapes, etc. Get the largest capacity pail that will slide under the drainage spout of the press.

Graf poly tank

CARBOYS. The number needed will depend on how many grapes you expect to be processing. One hundred pounds of grapes will yield roughly 6 gallons of unfermented must and pulp and 5 gallons of finished wine after loss of pulp and lees from several rackings. However, if you will be fermenting white wines and using carboys as primary fermenters, bear in mind that a 5-gallon carboy will accommodate only 60 to 70 pounds of grapes. That's because it can be filled only 3/4 full, taking foaming into consideration. And an extra carboy will be needed for racking purposes.

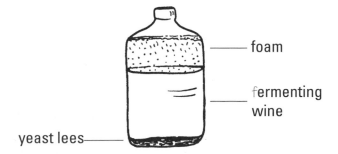

Carboys come in 13, 7, 6, 5, 3 and 2.8 gallon sizes, but some sizes are difficult to locate. After you have several 5-gallon carboys, get a 3-gallon carboy, or a 7-gallon carboy. You'll appreciate the flexibility year after year. You can never have too many carboys! Avoid plastic carboys as oxygen will eventually permeate and ruin the wine.

You will also need some smaller jugs to temporarily handle the excess volume — 1 gallon, 4 liter, 3 liter, 1.5 liter, etc. Make sure your stoppers will fit as the neck diameters of jugs vary.

CARBOY STOPPERS. You will need one solid stopper per carboy and one drilled air lock stopper per carboy. Size no. 7 fits most carboys; no. 6½ fits most jugs. Rubber stoppers are better than cork as they last indefinitely and don't lose their shape. Cork stoppers tend to assume the shape of the carboy neck and seat less dependably with age. Some stoppers made of newer synthetic materials, such as Dynaflex and Kraton, are elongated and will work in a wider range of neck diameters than rubber; they work well for gallon jugs. Stoppers can be wrapped with a layer of heavy plastic wrap to counter the tendency to back out. The type used by delis to wrap sandwiches works, as does Stretch-Tite® from Costco. Punch a hole in the plastic wrap if using an air lock so the gas can escape.

AIR LOCKS. Several types of air locks or "bubblers" are available; all work acceptably well as long as the water level is maintained. The two-piece air lock with a straight stem and separate float requires less headspace above the carboy. It can also be used with a ½" vinyl hose to displace the air in a carboy before racking (see *appendix C*). It has the disadvantage of drawing reservoir liquid into the wine if the temperature falls, causing the volume to shrink. The one-piece, "S-shaped" air lock allows for backflow of air without contaminating the wine with reservoir liquid.

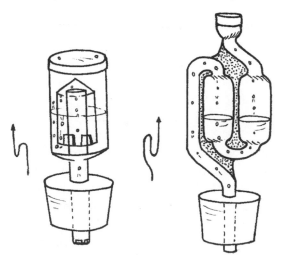

PLASTIC FUNNELS. Get the largest capacity you can find for racking into carboys. You will also need a smaller funnel to fit into wine bottles.

RACKING STEM, HOSE & CLIP. For racking from carboy to carboy, you will need a clear vinyl hose and racking stem of $5/16$", $3/8$" and/or $1/2$" diameter. If you get only one hose to begin with, the $3/8$" size would probably be best as it is good for both siphoning and bottling. The $1/2$" size is faster for racking and can also be used to funnel CO_2 from a fermenting carboy to an empty carboy to fill it with gas (see *appendix C)*. Plastic clips are made which slip over the $5/16$" diameter to cut off the flow.

HYDROMETER, JAR AND WINE THIEF. This is basic equipment for testing the level of unfermented sugar in musts and sugar solutions. A wine thief is a convenience for lifting samples out of carboys (see next page).

BRUSHES. A carboy brush and a bottle brush are indispensable. Bend the carboy brush to fit the shoulder of the carboy. I have a second carboy brush bent at 90 degrees to clean the bottoms.

WOOD DOWELS. This is a hardware store item. Used when stirring up lees to promote malolactic fermentation, for topping in fining agents or meta rather than racking, etc. I have a very slender one for stirring up MLF lees and a thicker one for heavier jobs.

MEDICINAL TEASPOON. The ordinary kitchen teaspoon is amazingly inaccurate! They are often 30% more or less than a true teaspoon, which is approximately 5 ml. Greater accuracy is needed for measuring chemicals such as tartaric acid and meta. Get a medicinal teaspoon at the drug store, which can be used by trial and error to find a kitchen teaspoon that happens to be accurate. Then mark the kitchen version and use it to measure your chemicals by volume — it's much easier than weighing every time.

ACID TEST KIT. Total acid is such an important measurement in winemaking that you should invest in an acid test kit early in your home winemaking career. It will be well worth the modest cost. See *appendix A* for details on assembling your own kit and conducting titration tests.

CLINITEST TABLETS. These tablets for measuring residual sugar are available at some drug stores if your wine shop does not carry them. They are particularly important in making white wines in which small quantities of residual sugar are desired. See *appendix A* for details on use.

PIPETS. Serological or graduated pipets are one of the most useful supply items. The 1 ml size can be used for Clinitest and for acid titration tests. When you are interested in controlling the addition of sulfite at bottling for instance, $1/4$ tsp. of potassium metabisulfite can be dissolved in 25 ml of water and 1 ml dispensed into each bottle to give 50 ppm. A 1 ml pipet can be used as a straw to sample wine right out of the carboy. I would suggest a 1-ml disposable pipet for measuring musts and two 1-ml class A pipets for titrations.

A volumetric pipet of 5 , 10 or 20 ml size is needed to measure wine samples when doing titration tests with a burette (see *appendix A*). They double as a wine thief! A lab supply house will normally carry pipets if your wine supply shop does not.

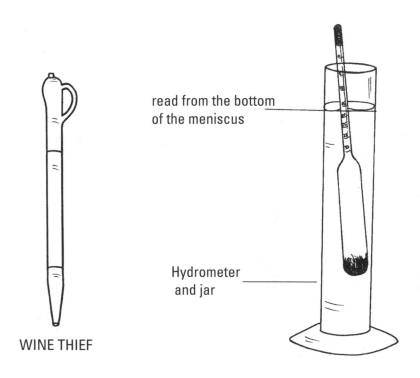

read from the bottom
of the meniscus

Hydrometer
and jar

WINE THIEF

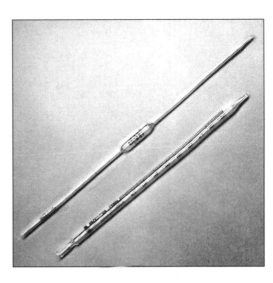

*Volumetric (top) and
serological pipets.*

(SCALE). Some type of scale capable of measuring fractions of an ounce (and preferably metric as well) is a convenience, but by no means a necessity. A photographer's, reloader's or digital postage scale would work, but you can get by without a scale. This book usually references chemicals in fractions of a teaspoon on the assumption that you will not have a scale.

(INERT GAS TANK AND REGULATOR). Although it is possible to use a "CO_2 pot" to generate an inert gas (see *appendix C*), you are not likely to do it every time, due to the nuisance factor. If you plan to ferment a lot of white wines, a tank of inert gas with a flow regulator is the answer to the air problem. White wines — and particularly those from hot climates — are so sensitive to air that every effort should be made to minimize the air contact. A tank makes it easy to displace the air. I have a small tank of argon with a regulator valve that reduces the flow to 20 cubic feet per hour. Argon is heavier than nitrogen or carbon dioxide and the molecules are larger, so it does not get absorbed as readily. With a tank of inert gas you can purge every carboy of air before racking into it. You can use it to protect wine in partially-filled carboys. The gas will protect the cap of red grapes during extended

Argon tank with regulator

maceration if replenished daily. I sometimes give each empty bottle a puff at bottling time. The cost at a welding supply shop was less than $100 filled, and a refill a year and a half later was only $15. While I would not classify a tank as a necessity, it has been one of my most satisfying equipment additions because it has so many uses.

(pH METER). Although it is not by any means a necessity, a pH meter will give you more insight into wine chemistry than any other piece of luxury equipment. You can quickly determine the effect on this all-important measurement of various procedures, such as increasing or decreasing the acid level, cold stabilization and malolactic fermentation, to name a few. See page 176 for more on digital pH meters.

Chemicals Glossary

POTASSIUM METABISULFITE. $1/4$ tsp/5 gal.= 50 parts per million (ppm); 1 t = 6.3 g. Some people are allergic to sulfite and asthmatics are particularly sensitive to it. The fumes are highly caustic and care should always be taken to avoid breathing it or getting the solution in your mouth. Despite these disadvantages, I regard potassium metabisulfite, also referred to as "sulfite" or "meta," as the winemaker's best friend! Its virtues are many and impressive. It kills unwanted bacteria and foreign yeast but not cultured yeast. It inhibits enzymatic browning of white wines. It promotes clarification after fermentation is over. It stabilizes a white wine with residual sugar and discourages renewed fermentation. It extends the shelf life of your wine, and at the right level, it actually improves the flavor. However, don't use it indiscriminately. Low levels of meta will provide all the benefits.

There is universal agreement among vintners around the world that sulfite is needed <u>after</u> fermentation. It not only kills microbial bacteria and other would-be spoilers, but it is also an antioxidant. The shelf life of a wine with normal pH and no sulfite will not be much more than one year, depending on the pH. The principal controversy is whether sulfite should be used <u>before</u> fermentation. Some winemakers use no sulfite until after fermentation in the belief that a more flavorful wine results. These folks, comprising the "brown school," will accept a bit of browning in exchange for the slightly greater complexity added by the natural yeast early in fermentation. The browning will disappear anyway during clarification. They hope for more complexity from the natural yeasts that would otherwise be killed by sulfite. And they also want to keep the acetaldehyde to an absolute minimum. Some acetaldehyde is always formed during fermentation, and sulfiting before fermentation will increase the level of acetaldehyde somewhat.

The "green school" counters that the natural yeast is killed by very low alcohol levels (5 - 6%), and there is no assurance that the by-products of wild yeast fermentation will benefit the wine anyway — they could be a negative. The green school wants to eliminate all forms of natural yeast and malolactic bacteria. They prefer to avoid all browning in favor of a clean fermentation with a predictable outcome. They don't care if the aldehyde level is marginally higher, since it is so low as to escape detection anyway.

Take your pick, but note that if sulfite is not used until after fermentation is complete, extra care should be taken in cleanliness before and during crushing, as the risk of spoilage goes up. Sulfite everything that comes in contact with the must or wine and then rinse the equipment with water. Discard overripe and spoiled clusters with greater care. I would never omit the sulfite with grapes having *botrytis,* mold, or high pH; in fact, more sulfite should be used.

Some winemakers like Campden tablets, which add about 75 ppm of sulfite at the rate of one tablet per gallon. They must be crushed with a mortar and pestle, and even then they are difficult to completely dissolve. The granular form of potassium metabisulfite is easier to use and less expensive.

Meta loses its strength over time and should be tightly capped and replaced every year. Use last year's meta for making a cleaning solution. See *appendix I* for technical data on the exacting use of potassium metabisulfite in relation to pH and use of a 10% stock solution.

TANNIN. Since white grapes have little or no tannin, some winemakers like to add a very small quantity ($1/4$ to $1/2$ tsp per 5 gallons) of tannin for astringency and as an aid in later fining with gelatin or isinglass.

PECTIC ENZYME. Pectic enzyme is commonly used in making fruit wines from apricots, peaches and other pit fruits. It can also be used for grape wines. It increases the yield of white grapes by breaking down the pulp and makes pressing more efficient. It aids in extracting flavors from the skins of red grapes by accelerating physical disintegration of the berry. Pectic enzyme loses it potency over time, so keep it refrigerated and replace it every 2 years. Follow manufacturer's recommended dosage. Note that enzymes will be rendered ineffective if bentonite is added at the same time.

POTASSIUM BITARTRATE. 1 tsp/gal. Used as seed to hasten tartrate crystallization when cold stabilizing. Dissolve it in a quart of wine and stir it into the carboy with a dowel when the wine is at its coldest.

POTASSIUM SORBATE. Although it will not stop active fermentation, potassium sorbate will insure against renewed fermentation in wines bottled with higher levels of unfermented sugar. Add it at the rate of $3/4$ grams per gallon (200 ppm) and use it in conjunction with potassium metabisulfite for maximum effectiveness. It has a distinct flavor which some people dislike. Potassium sorbate is not needed for ordinary table wines having residual sugar of less than 1%. However, if the grapes had *botrytis cinerea* and the wine is being bottled with 3% residual sugar, it can be used as insurance against renewed fermentation. Potassium sorbate will generate a geranium-like odor disagreeable to most people if it is present during malolactic fermentation. See notes at page 102 to completely eliminate the need for potassium sorbate.

There are Glossaries after several succeeding chapters which should also be consulted:

Chapter Two

Fermenting White Table Wines

he basic process for making white table wines is as simple as it is universal. After the grapes are crushed and pressed, the juice is fermented in an enclosed container, free of air. Home winemakers typically ferment their white wines in partially-filled carboys topped with an air lock. After most of the sugar has been fermented and the frothy stage of fermentation is past, the carboys are topped up and allowed to ferment to complete dryness. After it is dry, the wine is clarified, the residual sugar and total acid are corrected, and it is bottled. The commercial winery will filter at least once in addition to gravity fining, and it may age the wine in oak casks for a period of time. But the basic procedure is otherwise the same for both.

Sterilizing solution

The first step in the new fermenting season should be the preparation of a jug of sulfite solution. It is easier to always have a jug of sterilizing solution ready when racking or cleaning equipment than having to mix a new solution every time. It will be used repeatedly throughout the season. The exact concentration is not critical, so start with 3 tablespoons of potassium metabisulfite and an optional 3 tablespoons of citric acid dissolved in a gallon of water. I get fresh meta every year because it deteriorates. (Use last year's meta to make cleaning solutions.) The solution can be reused; after rinsing out a carboy, for instance, just funnel it back into the jug. When it gets low, top it up with more water and meta. If it picks up too much sediment, mix a new solution.

This is also the time to make a 10% solution of potassium metabisulfite if you want to avoid having to measure and dissolve a fractional teaspoon for each addition. I recommend a 10% solution because it is easier and is probably less prone to error (see page 219).

Culling out bad fruit

Before being crushed, the grapes should be examined carefully and any rotten clusters discarded. If a cluster is raisined and hard, discard it and proceed using only fruit that is of sound quality. Sometimes there will not be a bad cluster in the whole lot; at other times, culling out the bad fruit can be tedious. But it is important with white wines. Resist the temptation to wash the fruit as it probably would not remove any residual sprays and would only set the stage for unwanted mold and infection.

Preparing a yeast starter solution

A yeast starter solution should be initiated as soon as the grapes or juice arrive. Spontaneous or "natural" fermentation—the process of crushing and pressing without sulfite and letting natural yeast on the grapes and in the air establish and do the fermenting—is fashionable with some commercial vintners. But it's not recommended for the home winemaker, particularly with white wines. It takes too long for natural yeast to multiply to the point where they start converting the sugar to alcohol, and the result is too uncertain. In addition, most strains of wild yeast will not ferment to complete dryness because they are killed off by low alcohol levels. Use one of the many strains of cultured wine yeast and you will get better results.

There are two steps involved in building a yeast starter solution, the first being to activate the packet of dry yeast. Start with $1/2$ cup of warm water—about 90° F (32° C). Sprinkle the yeast granules over the surface, without stirring. It will be rehydrated in minutes.

The second step is increasing the volume. This is best done by squeezing or mashing up a cup of fresh grape juice and diluting it with a cup of water to lower the sugar level. (Diluted because yeast multiply faster with medium sugar concentration than high). Add a pinch of diammonium phosphate ("D.A.P.") to stimulate multiplication. Mix the yeast cup and diluted grape juice together in a carafe or jar, plug it with cheesecloth and set it atop the hot water heater or in a warm window sill. This should all be accomplished within 15–30 minutes after the yeast was initially hydrated. The starter solution will be actively fermenting in an hour or two.

The $1^1/_2$ pints of yeast starter solution thus concocted will be sufficient to inoculate 10 gallons of must at the optimum starter-to-must ratio of 2%. A larger volume of starter could be used, but that would needlessly dilute the wine. If you have more than 10 gallons of must to ferment and need more than $1^1/_2$ pint of starter, start with 2 or 3 cups of fresh juice, dilute with an equal volume of water, and follow the same procedure. Always wait until the starter is fermenting actively before inoculating.

Normally, one prefers to work with dry yeasts as they are easier. However, some excellent yeast strains exist which are available only in liquid form. The procedure for activating a liquid yeast is basically the same, but it might take longer to become active to the point where it can be used to inoculate the must. With a slow-fermenting liquid yeast sample, such as Steinberg, start two or three days before the grapes are to arrive. You want the starter to be active and ready to go when the grapes are crushed and pressed so as to minimize the delay before fermentation.

Start with $1/2$ cup of freshly-pressed juice from oranges, grapefruits or Thompson seedless grapes and dilute with $1/2$ cup of water. Don't use canned or pasteurized juices as they might contain preservatives which would inhibit yeast growth. Bring the diluted juice to a brief boil to kill the wild yeast. After it has cooled, add a pinch of D.A.P. and the liquid yeast sample. Cover the carafe or jar with cheesecloth and set it in a warm place. It might take a couple of days, but it will eventually become active. It helps after about 24 hours to pour it back and forth into another container for aeration. Yeast like air during the multiplication stage. (But when they reach maximum concentration and start converting the sugar to alcohol, air should be eliminated).

When the grapes arrive, add a cup of the freshly-pressed grape juice plus a cup of water to increase the volume. Put it back in the warm spot until it is active again and ready to add to the must a few hours later.

Of course, if you already have wine fermenting and want to use the same strain of yeast for the next batch of grapes, it's even easier to get a starter. Just siphon a cup or two of the lees off the bottom of the fermenting must and add it to some fresh grape juice diluted with water. It will be active shortly.

Cleanliness

Cleanliness is important, but not in the sense that a beginning winemaker might expect. Don't worry about a few earwigs and spiders! They'll end up in the lees just like the dead yeast cells. Nor is a little dirt any cause for concern. My point is not to encourage a disregard of cleanliness, but to emphasize the principal concern of a home winemaker—AIR. Without air as the catalyst, most dirt, bacteria and other potential sources of spoilage remain innocuous. If you want to be a fanatic about something, let it be air rather than dirt. Minimize air contact at all times and you are not likely to experience spoilage problems.

Yes, the equipment should be clean, but it need not be surgically sterile. If the crusher and press were cleaned after the last use and show no signs of mold, it will suffice to hose them down. If they look dirty, they should be scrubbed and then sprayed with some of your sulfite cleaning solution in a hand sprayer. Some winemakers religiously sulfite everything that comes in contact with their wine. But if my equipment is clean, I normally just hose it down and have not had problems with spoilage. That's probably because I use sulfite at crushing and am a fanatic about air.

Crushing

The grapes should be crushed as soon as possible after being picked and fermentation initiated with as little delay as possible.

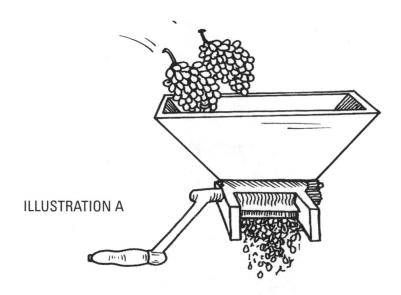

ILLUSTRATION A

If they were picked late in the day and are warm, cool them over-night and crush in the morning. More flavor will be retained if crushed cool. White grapes should be crushed on the stems as the stems stabilize the mass in the press and facilitate drainage of the juice. A simple crusher with two rollers, mounted over a primary fermenter or other receptacle, is all that one needs for crushing white grapes *(Illustration A)*. If you have a crusher-stemmer, re-move the de-stemming trough. If you cannot disable the de-stemmer, mix some stems back in before pressing.

After crushing, the grapes go into a large pail or primary fer-menter of food grade quality. A small amount of potassium metabisulfite, or "meta" as I usually refer to it, is carefully mea-sured, dissolved in an ounce or two of water and thoroughly mixed in. The dosage will depend on the condition of the grapes.

For grapes in good condition having normal sugar, acid and pH, the recommended dosage of meta is $1/4$ tsp per 5 gallons of vol-ume, which is roughly 50 parts per million (ppm). If you mixed a 10% solution of meta (page 219), add 3.32 ml per U.S. gallon (.88 ml per liter) to get 50 ppm. If your grapes are high in sugar, low in acid and presumably have a high pH, the dosage should be in-creased to 100 ppm. Use of more than 120 ppm is not advisable unless the grapes are badly sunburned, have broken skins, bunchrot or are in extremely poor condition, which hopefully will

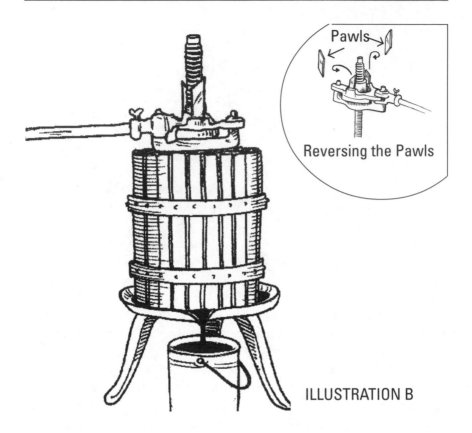

Pawls

Reversing the Pawls

ILLUSTRATION B

not be the case.

Contrary to its current image, meta is a great preservative and antioxidant and will help keep the must from browning. It kills natural yeast and bacteria but has little effect on cultured yeast at levels under 50 ppm. Don't hesitate to use it. On the other hand, never use more than necessary. Keep accurate records as to how much meta was added to each batch of wine and when. Be aware that an unfermented must will accommodate more meta than a finished wine. And a wine will handle larger doses of meta right after fermentation, when it still contains solids, than it will after clarification. In my experience judging at county fairs, excess meta is the most common mistake of home winemakers. They add too much, too late in the game.

Some winemakers also add pectic enzyme at the time the grapes are crushed as it will hasten maceration of the berries and increase the volume of liquid. I prefer not to use it because it also increases the volume of pulp, which should not be fermented. I question whether the yield is increased much at all after the pulp is settled and the juice racked off. Since I suspect that pectic enzyme makes clarification more difficult, I no longer use it on white wines.

Pressing

Dip the crushed grapes and juice out of the primary fermenter with a small pail and pour them into the press basket. It is not necessary to line the basket with cheesecloth or fiberglass mesh in pressing *vinifera* grapes, but one certainly could, as is commonly done in pressing the very slippery *labrusca* grapes. Compact the mass as much as possible by hand, then add more grapes, compress by hand again. When the basket is nearly full, place the wood blocks and screw in position and start applying mechanical pressure. When you meet stiff resistance and the flow diminishes to a trickle, take a break. Have another sip of last year's effort! The flow will stop completely in a few minutes and then you can start cranking again. Repeat the cycle of pressing and waiting until it has been pressed to your satisfaction.

When it has been fully pressed, reverse the pawls (*Illustration B inset*), back off the screw and remove the blocks. Then discard the pomace. Reassemble the basket and repeat the process.

The grapes can actually be pressed two or three times to maximize the yield—fluff them up and start over. Additional pressings are certainly worthwhile if you press whole clusters without crushing first in order to minimize skin contact, or if your press is inefficient due to its large capacity. The grapes in the center of the mass will still contain some juice. However, additional pressings will not increase the yield very much if you use a small press, crush the grapes, use pectic enzyme and soak on the skins before pressing; you will get almost all of the fermentable juice with one hard pressing.

You will get a better wine by settling out the pulp and fermenting only the clear juice (see chapter 10).

Adding yeast starter

Since the goal is to get fermentation under way as quickly as possible, the must should be inoculated as soon as the yeast starter is active. The only caveat is that inoculation should be delayed for 30 minutes after sulfiting to give the sulfite time to bond with the solids and impurities in the must. Cultured yeasts are somewhat sensitive to sulfite, but after a few minutes they will not be affected. However, if you had to give your grapes an unusually heavy dose of meta because they were in poor condition, wait several hours before inoculating.

If your starter is not visibly active by the time you are through crushing, store the must in a cool place while waiting for the starter to become so. It's a good idea to keep a couple of gallon ice jugs ready in the freezer in case you run into an extended delay in getting your starter active—just tighten the caps, drop the jugs in and stir the must occasionally to cool it throughout.

To inoculate, just sprinkle the starter solution over the surface of the must. This allows air contact, which stimulates yeast multiplication. Don't stir it, as that would disperse the concentration of yeast, reduce exposure to air and slow down multiplication. After you see signs of fermentation, it can be stirred if you wish. Even then, stirring is not necessary.

Since white grapes are low in nutrients, some winemakers add a balanced yeast food, D.A.P., yeast hulls, yeast extract, or the like when pressing (one teaspoon per 5 U.S. gallons). I do this with Chardonnay grapes from California, which are said to be the most nutrient-deficient of the white varieties. I also add yeast food if I suspect that the grapes have residual sulfur on the skins. The nitrogen in the yeast food reduces the tendency to generate H_2S toward the end of fermentation. Yeast food is generally not necessary for *vinifera* grapes, but it is good insurance against stuck fermentation. If fermentation is reluctant to start, it is almost always the result of too much sulfite, inoculating before the starter is fully active or low temperature rather than lack of nutrients.

Temperature is a major consideration when attempting to initiate fermentation. Since yeast multiply faster under warm conditions, the temperature should be maintained at 65-70° F (18-21° C) until fermentation starts. The temperature can be lowered after fermentation is underway if you want to cold ferment. I usually initiate fermentation of white wines at room temperature and then move the carboys outdoors once it starts. It takes longer, but cold fermentation will produce a better white wine (see chapter 10).

Testing total acid and sugar

The sugar and acidity of the must should be tested as soon after pressing as possible. Always take and record these two readings — after pressing but before fermentation starts (see *appendix A*). A hydrometer is the only item needed to check the sugar level. The sugar content of white wine grapes should be in the range of 18° – 24° Brix, depending on the variety.

A titration test kit for testing total acid is inexpensive and easy to use. The total titratable acid would ideally be between 6 to 9 grams/liter before fermentation. I usually refer to acid readings as percentages, such as .6% or .9%, which would be 6 or 9 grams per liter. (See *appendix A* for details on conducting titration tests).

Adjusting acid level

Hopefully, the acid level of the must will be in the desired range and adjustments will not be needed. But sometimes, due to weather or timing of the pick, the acid level will be off. In hot climates, the sugar level can shoot past the desired level in one or two days, resulting in low acid. In any climate, rain or unseasonably cold weather can hamper ripening so that sugar and acid never do reach the desired levels. Humidity can cause mold and force premature harvesting. There are several ways to raise acidity (chapter 8) and several ways to lower it (chapter 9).

The acid level of the finished wine should be a minimum of .55%, up to a maximum of .70%. Ideally, it would be .60–.65%. If the acid level of the must is low, it should be adjusted right now. The lower the acid, the more important that it be raised before fermentation rather than after. If you do not adjust before fermentation and end up having to raise it by more than .15–.20% afterward, the resulting wine will eventually show a harshness after bottling, due to the artificial acid. If the acid is added before, it will integrate with the natural acids during fermentation and be less noticeable. In other words, you can make a much larger adjustment before fermentation. In addition, there is less tendency for bitartrate crystals to precipitate if the acid is adjusted before. I have fermented many

West Coast musts with good results where the acid was .4%, or even lower. But I always add the acid before fermentation.

Since acid drops somewhat during fermentation and cold stabilization, you might even want to raise the acid slightly above the desired level in the finished wine. However, if your grapes are significantly overripe, it is probably better to add the minimum amount of acid and plan to accept a lower acid level in the finished wine, say .55% – .60%.

An excess of acid will also have to be corrected, but it is less critical that it be done before fermentation. Two of the options are the same — blending or chemicals. There is a third option for some types of white wines, such as Chardonnay and Sauvignon Blanc — malolactic fermentation. If total acid in the must exceeds 0.9 – 1.0%, the commentary in chapter 9 will be helpful in deciding on the corrective action to take now. My rule of thumb is never to start fermentation of a white wine with acid in excess of 1.0%.

Adjusting sugar

The practice of adding sugar, known as chaptalization, is common in Germany and other regions where grapes have difficulty ripening and sometimes have to be picked with sugar as low as 17° Brix. Whether or not sugar should be added depends on the level of natural sugar in the must, the grape type and the style of wine to be made. If you are crushing Chardonnay or Sauvignon Blanc grapes with low sugar and want a dry table wine, the sugar should be raised to 20° or 21° Brix. Just stir it in — 1½ ounces of ordinary table sugar per gallon will raise the Brix by 1°. This can be done at your leisure while waiting for fermentation to commence, or even shortly after fermentation starts. High quality concentrates are a very good alternative to table sugar for raising sugar levels.

The sugar level is less critical in the case of other white grapes, such as Riesling, Gewurztraminer and Semillon, particularly if your goal is a semisweet wine. But even then, I would raise the sugar level by 1° or 2° if it is below 18° B. after crushing and pressing.

If the acid level is low, the sugar is probably high. I have successfully fermented white grapes with Brix of 28° Brix by adding water to lower the sugar to 24° B. and then adding tartaric acid to raise total acid to .55 – .60%. Even if the acid were close to normal, adding water will dilute the existing acid and give rise to the need for a new titration test.

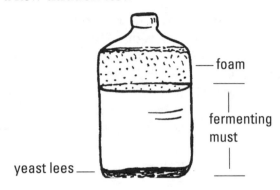

foam

fermenting must

yeast lees

Fermenting in carboys

At some point, the must will be poured into carboys. Some wine-makers let it ferment two or three days in an open primary fer-menter before transferring to carboys. My preference is to transfer as soon as fermentation starts. The carboys should be filled only three-fourths full. The air space is needed to allow room for foam-ing. A certain amount of foaming always accompanies fermenta-tion, but it can be quite dramatic with certain vigorous yeasts un-der warm conditions and in musts containing large amounts of pulp. Note that fermentation could also be initiated in the carboy (³⁄₄ full), but it will take longer to start because the must has less exposure to air. You might have to aerate it if fermentation is re-luctant to start.

Fermentation should start in 24 to 36 hours; if not, see *appendix B*. Once fermentation starts, the must should be deprived of oxy-gen. In fact, avoidance of air contact should become your guiding principle from now until the wine is finally bottled and corked in six or eight months. Substitute an air lock for the cheesecloth. Pour sulfite solution in the reservoir of the air lock to help discourage the fruit flies.

Controlling fermentation

After fermentation starts, the goal changes. Whereas the initial goal was to get fermentation initiated as quickly as possible, now the goal is to avoid "runaway" fermentation. If a vigorous yeast is used under warm fermenting conditions, it could ferment to complete dryness in 3 or 4 days. That's too fast — too much of the bouquet and complexity is lost. Overly vigorous fermentation can be avoided by using a slower yeast or by lowering the temperature of the must.

The ideal temperature range for fermenting most white wines is 50–60° F (10-16° C). In this range, it will take ten days or more for the sugar to ferment down to 10° B. At this slower rate, the loss of bouquet is minimized and more of the fruit flavor is retained. When deciding where to ferment, look for the coolest place you can find. If you do not have an air conditioned corner of the house, the basement would be fine. Garages are often used but they can get hot in the fall. I frequently ferment white wines outside on the north side of the house, out of the direct sunlight. However, if temperatures in the range of 80-90° F (24-32° C) are encountered, a way should be found to cool the must.

Fermentation will start rather slowly, but will quickly gather momentum. The most vigorous fermentation will occur when the sugar is dropping from 20° Brix to 10° Brix. Fermentation should be monitored twice daily during this stage. Lift a sample out of the carboy with a wine thief. If the sugar level appears to be falling by more than 5° per day as fermentation speeds up, find a way to cool it. You could make a cold water bath by setting the carboys in a tub or wading pool with running tap water. If your tap water is too warm, drop in a block of ice or milk jugs with frozen water once or twice a day. It is only the extreme afternoon heat that is cause for concern as the night air will cool.

Once the sugar level drops below 10° B., you can relax. The frothy, tumultuous stage is over. With the higher alcohol content and lowered sugar level, fermentation will slow no matter what the temperature or what the yeast type.

Always be alert to possible "rotten egg" smell during or after fermentation, which indicates hydrogen sulfide. Immediate corrective action should be taken if it is encountered (see *appendix B*). Note, however, that some yeasts, most notably Montrachet, will generate a mild hydrogen sulfide odor. This is usually not a problem as it will disappear after one or two rackings. It is a pronounced and unmistakable rotten egg odor that is cause for concern.

Combining carboys

When the hydrometer indicates that unfermented sugar is approaching $0°$ Brix, the carboys should be combined and filled to the top. There will still be around 2% unfermented sugar when the hydrometer reads $0°$ Brix. You want the carboys to be full when the wine falls still and CO_2 is no longer being produced to dispel air. If the unsightly muck on the neck and shoulders of the carboy doesn't bother you, just top up — the muck might look gross but will not affect wine quality. It would be equally acceptable to rack into clean carboys.

Unless H_2S was encountered, you can use the "mud" and pulp on the bottom if more liquid is needed to fill the last carboy. It's also acceptable to top up with a similar wine of good quality. There will seldom be any defects in a wine at this early stage, but note that it is always good practice to taste each carboy before two different lots are blended or combined. If one happened to have flaws, both batches would probably be ruined by blending.

Juggle the volumes as needed to fill a lesser number of carboys. As a result of combining carboys, three fermenting carboys will become two; or four will become three, as the case may be. This is where it becomes convenient to have carboys in a variety of sizes, such as 2.8, 3, 5 and 7 gallon sizes. A few jugs and larger bottles — 1 gallon, 3 liter, 4 liter, 1.5 liter — should also have been located ahead of time to accommodate the excess volume. Top the jugs with an air lock and allow them to ferment to dryness along with the carboys. Small, drilled air lock stoppers are made which will even allow you to ferment in wine bottles. Every container should be as full as possible so as to minimize air contact. The smallest container can be topped with water if necessary. The point is to take no chances with air.

This is also a good time to add a little tannin, which white grapes lack. If you plan to add oak chips of some type, the tannin in the oak will be sufficient. If not, $1/4$ to $1/2$ tsp. of tannin per 5 gallons could be added, first dissolved in an ounce or two of water. This small amount will add a bit of astringency to the wine and will be helpful in later clarification efforts involving isinglass or gelatin. If malolactic fermentation is on your agenda, you can add the starter now, being sure to maintain a temperature of 65° F (18° C) or more until the process is complete. See chapter 12 — *Malolactic Fermentation.*

After the carboys have been combined, the wine should be allowed to ferment to dryness. Since this might take several weeks at temperatures below 60° F (16° C), I normally finish fermentation at room temperature. This not only assures uninterrupted and complete fermentation but saves several weeks of fermenting time and allows for earlier bottling. A warmer temperature is also needed to support malolactic fermentation if that is desired. If you have been cold fermenting outside, this would mean lugging the carboys inside.

Raising the temperature is not a necessity as the wine will usually ferment to dryness but over a longer period. But note that a nearly finished wine should not be subjected to temperatures below 50° F (10° C) for an extended period of time. It might get "stuck" with a few points of unfermented sugar, and it could be difficult to re-initiate fermentation in the spring.

The wine will normally be dry when the bubbles stop, but this should be confirmed with Clinitest *(see appendix A)*. Clinitest tablets are the only practical way to check residual sugar; a hydrometer will not accurately measure unfermented sugar because the alcohol level has altered the density of the liquid. You cannot rely on your palate right after fermentation as the wine is still too yeasty. Clinitest is the answer. As long as the residual sugar is below .1% or .2% (dark blue-green on the Clinitest chart), consider it dry, even though trace amounts of various unfermented sugars will always remain.

Settling the gross lees

After fermentation is complete, the carboys should be topped up again if necessary and left undisturbed for three or four weeks in a cool corner of the garage or basement while the dead yeast cells, pectins and various by-products of fermentation, called the "gross lees," settle out. The wine will be racked and fined several times over the next six months or so to promote clarification. But first, the gross lees should be allowed to settle out.

After the carboys have been combined and all effervescence has stopped, replace the air lock with a solid rubber stopper. Although not mandatory, it is good practice to wrap the stopper with a sticky plastic wrap of the type delicatessens use to wrap sandwiches. This will help hold the stopper firmly in place. If the stopper keeps popping out, this is a signal that microbes are busy at work, converting H_2S into mercaptans and disulfides. The minute volume of gas produced by this process cannot be detected with an air lock, but it will often force a stopper out. A popped stopper is a good indicator of unwanted activity — see *appendix B*. After three or four weeks, the gross lees will have settled and clarification will have come to a standstill, and the wine will be ready for the first racking.

Of course, if you are attempting to put the wine through malolactic fermentation, you would use an air lock rather than a stopper and try to hold the temperature at 70–75° F (21-24° C) until MLF is complete.

Yeasts Glossary

Many different strains of yeast are readily available to the home winemaker. Lallemand, Gist-brocades and Red Star collectively dominate the market. Vierka also markets an extensive line of dry and liquid yeasts, but many cannot be identified beyond the marketing name, such as "Sauternes." Although I have found the yeasts to be dependable, the nomenclature could be misleading to someone inclined to assume that the yeast type will determine the wine type. Nothing could be further from the truth.

Much has been written about the different flavor characteristics that various strains of yeasts impart. Differences undoubtedly exist immediately after fermentation, and they matter greatly to a commercial winery not wanting to tie up its fermentation capacity too long and wanting its wines to be marketable as soon as possible. But the differences are minor from the home winemaker's viewpoint. Two years after a wine has been bottled, I doubt whether anyone would be able to tell the difference.

Selection of yeast strain is nevertheless interesting and sometimes can be important. If, for instance, the Brix of the must is abnormally high, and you want a dry wine, pick a strain that is tolerant of high alcohol, such as Prise de Mousse or Pasteur Champagne. Do not use Epernay 2 as it is not very tolerant of high alcohol. If the grapes have *botrytis cinerea*, higher levels of sulfite should be used. Since the Brix will probably be higher, use one which is tolerant of high sulfite and high alcohol, like Prise de Mousse. If you want to cold ferment a white wine, use a cold-tolerant yeast, such as Epernay 2, Prise de Mousse or, my preference, Steinberg. If you want to stop fermentation with some residual sugar, use a less vigorous strain, which would again be Steinberg or Epernay 2, and deprive it of nutrients as well. If you suspect that the grapes have residual sulfur on them, do not use Montrachet as it is particularly prone to converting the sulfur into hydrogen sulfide.

Here is a brief description of the more common strains, including marketing names and the U.C. Davis number where applicable.

PRISE DE MOUSSE (Red Star, Premier Cuvée; Lalvin, EC1118). This vigorous dry yeast is good for either reds or whites, including cooler fermenting temperatures. It has become very popular with commercial wineries due to its willingness to ferment to completion with few problems. It has little effect on the varietal characteristic of the grape, which can be either a positive or negative, depending on the result desired. It settles well and is a good choice for barrel fermentation. Prise de Mousse is a good yeast to re-initiate a stuck fermentation and for *tirage* fermentation of sparkling wines because it is tolerant of alcohol and sulfite. It is a very low foamer and does not have the tendency of Montrachet to generate hydrogen sulfide. However, it might be more difficult to initiate malolactic fermentation if this yeast is used.

MONTRACHET (UCD #522) is quite vigorous and produces a finished wine, red or white, with excellent complexity. It remains one of my favorites for red wines, Chardonnay and even Gewurztraminer. However, it is prone to produce hydrogen sulfide, particularly if the grapes had residual sulfur on them.

PASTEUR RED This is an excellent general purpose yeast for full-bodied red wines, such as Cabernet Sauvignon and red Rhone varieties. It produces full-bodied, complex wines and has been a standard of commercial wineries for many years.

PASTEUR CHAMPAGNE (UCD #595). This is an all-purpose yeast commonly used for white wines. It is not used to make sparkling wines, however. It has good vigor, is quite tolerant of sulfite and leaves a pleasant yeasty flavor. It generates moderate foam.

PASTEUR WHITE (Red Star, French White). This yeast is used to make austere, complex white wines. It is a high foamer, so be sure to leave plenty of head space in the carboy.

EPERNAY 2 (Red Star, Côtes de Blanc). This medium-speed yeast emphasizes the fruit in either reds or whites. Epernay is sometimes used to ferment Rieslings or Gewurztraminers intended to have some residual sugar as it tends not to ferment all the way to dryness at cool temperatures (i.e., it tends to get stuck late in fermentation). It is not very tolerant of high alcohol levels. Add 1 tsp. per 5 U.S. gallons of diammoniun phosphate if you want to ferment to complete dryness. It often leaves a "soapy" taste shortly after fermentation which will eventually dissipate.

STEINBERG (Geisenheim Inst.) ferments slowly and is ideal for cold fermenting a white wine over a long period of time. It produces a wine with good complexity and structure. It is my favorite for cool fermentation of white wines. It slows, but does not completely stop at temperatures below 50° F (10° C). One disadvantage, if you want to leave some residual sugar, is that it takes a couple of rackings and perhaps a fining to get it to stop fermenting. Take advantage of its sensitivity to sulfite by adding 50 ppm at the second racking, when it should be almost still. I have not seen Steinberg in 5-gram packets, but the Wyeast pouch is a source.

LALLEMAND (http://www.lallemand.com) markets five of its popular Lalvin yeasts in 5-gram packets:

Lalvin EC 1118. Same as Prise de Mousse above.

Lalvin D-47. Used primarily for white wines. Very vigorous, produces wines with good mouth feel.

Lalvin RC 212. Classic strain for Pinot Noir, as it provides good color extraction and emphasizes the fruit and spicy quality of the grape.

Lalvin 71-B. This is an interesting yeast because it is claimed to neutralize up to 30% of the malic acid. It is a low foaming strain, which is often used to emphasize aroma and fruitiness in blush wines.

Lalvin K-1. Recommended for Sauvignon Blanc, French hybrid whites and light reds. It is claimed to retain fresh fruit aromas longer than standard yeasts.

WYEAST LABS (http://www.wyeastlab.com) of Mt. Hood, Oregon has a line of liquid yeasts in foil pouches ("Vintners Choice") that are easy to activate. The line includes 12 strains at last count, including Steinberg and Assmanhausen.

Many other excellent strains of yeast have been isolated, but are available only in 500 g. packages. Enoferm (Australian line) had 42 strains at last count! In addition to the 5 strains available in 5-gram packets, Lallemand has at least 26 other strains in its Laffort & Cie, Lalvin and Uvaferm lines. Gist-brocades (http://www.dsm.nl) markets about 12 different yeast strains, including the popular Fermirouge, Fermiblanc and Fermivin strains.

Note that "dry" does not mean freeze-dried; so don't put your yeasts in the freezer as you would freeze-dried malolactic packets. Dry yeasts store best at cool temperatures, such as the wine cellar.

Yeast Supplements Glossary

DIAMMONIUM PHOSPHATE (D.A.P.) $1/2 - 3/4$ g per gallon (.13–.20 g/L). 1 tsp. = 4.3 g. The legal limit of this nitrogen source is 3.6 g. per gallon (.95 g/L), but much less will suffice. It is very effective in stimulating yeast growth but usually is not necessary. It is good for making yeast starter solutions and in musts that are nutrient deficient, such as musts that have been pre-fined and settled before fermentation. A dose of D.A.P. when inoculating adds a bit of insurance against hydrogen sulfide if the grapes had residual sulfur on the skins. D.A.P. is generally recommended for California Chardonnay grapes and a good case can be made for using it in all fermentations. Malolactic bacteria cannot use D.A.P. as a nutrient source.

YEAST EXTRACT $1/2$ g per gallon (.13 g/L). This is a very good source of nitrogen for budding yeast cells. Malolactic bacteria like yeast extract as well.

YEAST HULLS, or "ghosts." 1.3 g per gallon (.34 g/L). This is the cell membranes of yeast — the innards became yeast extract. The hulls affect some of the acids in a way that promotes fermentation and reduces any tendency toward hydrogen sulfide production. Yeast hulls also promote malolactic fermentation and are helpful in re-starting a stuck primary fermentation.

BALANCED YEAST FOOD. Various blends of the above are marketed. They usually contain yeast vitamins as well, such as B-1, thiamin and vitamin H. I only use this more expensive supplement on the rare occasions when I need to reinoculate a stuck fermentation or when I know the vineyard to be deficient in nitrogen.

Chapter Three

BULK AGING

he wine will continue to be "bulk aged" for several months until it is clarified and bottled in late spring. In the meantime, it will be racked occasionally and fined with clarifying agents. Bulk aging is an important phase in the life cycle of a wine because it allows the vintner to check and re-check the total acid, pH and residual sugar readings and to make repeated taste evaluations. Increasingly smaller adjustments to the acid level will be made to nudge the wine closer to the desired objective. Several months are needed to make these evaluations and adjustments because right after fermentation, the yeast and tannins are so overwhelming as to interfere with taste evaluation. In a few months, however, the yeast flavor will start to subside and the tannins to soften. By bottling time, you will have a good sense of the wine you are working with. This is the principal benefit of bulk aging — a chance to get to know your product better and improve it!

Here is a racking and fining sequence that I have used with excellent results in clarifying white wines. It assumes bulk aging in glass or stainless steel vessels, not in oak barrels.

- The wine falls still and the gross lees are allowed to precipitate for 3 or 4 weeks.
- The wine is racked off the gross lees, fined with bentonite and given a dose of potassium metabisulfite.
- The wine is racked again, fined with isinglass, and cold stabilized for several weeks.
- The wine is racked for a third time, with the acid, residual sugar and sulfite being adjusted for the last time before bottling.
- The wine is bottled.

At each racking — and perhaps in between — you will be doing taste evaluations and titration tests to determine the acid level. Hopefully, with the corrections to total acid made before fermentation, the acid will be within the desired range, which can run from a low of .55% for a dry white table wine to a high of 70%. I consider .60 –.65% to be optimum. If the acid is high or low, you should start the correction process at the first racking and make small adjustments at subsequent rackings.

Bulk aging is also the time to focus on the balance between total acid and residual sugar. Most people like red table wines totally dry but not necessarily white table wines. A bone-dry white wine having residual sugar of less than .1% might seem well balanced at a very young age. This is because the fruitiness in a new wine has the same effect on the palate as sugar — it counters the acidity. But as the fruitiness diminishes over time, a bone-dry white wine will become too astringent for some people. A bit of residual sugar will keep it softer and fruitier and will be appreciated after the wine has aged a while. It also enhances the bouquet and brings out more of the varietal characteristic of the grapes.

The optimum amount of residual sugar will vary with the level of acid, the mix of acids, the pH, the grape type, and your personal preference. Titration readings, while helpful, do not tell the whole story. A wine with lower pH, for instance, will require slightly more residual sugar to balance it than one having the same total acid but higher pH. Similarly, some wines with acidity of .65%, for example, will taste more tart than others having the same acidity (and the same residual sugar). This is because the ratio of the various acids differs from wine to wine, and some acids taste more sour than others. In addition, a varying portion of the total acidity will be attributable to tartrate salts, which are less sour than tartaric acid itself. These variables make the residual sugar decision as much a matter of art as science, even for a commercial vintner. Rely on your tastes buds as much as the titration readings when deciding on the level of residual sugar. And remember that the wine will taste more tart as the fruitiness diminishes with age.

Here are some very general parameters for your initial guidance in balancing residual sugar (RS) and total acid. With a finished white table wine having total acidity in the .65 – .70% range, few people could distinguish between .1% RS and .4% RS; both would taste "dry" to most people. Unless you know that you like your white table wines bone dry, the minimum level of residual sugar should probably be around .2 or .3%, assuming normal acid. But again, it will depend on the grape type. Chardonnay, Sauvignon Blanc and Semillon, for instance, are often bottled drier than other varieties. If you like your wines with noticeable sweetness, you might want residual sugar of .75 – 1.00%, or possibly higher. This would be very appropriate for a Gewurztraminer or Riesling.

Given the absence of any hard and fast rules for balancing residual sugar and total acidity, I highly recommend the routine testing of the various commercial wines that you like, as well as your own. Keep notes for future reference as they will help you define your palate and facilitate a better guess as to how much residual sugar a particular wine should have.

Chapter Four

First Racking

 oward the end of fermentation, the partially-filled carboys were combined and topped up. After fermentation stopped, the gross lees were allowed to settle for three or four weeks. The wine is now much clearer but is still visibly hazy and has ceased to clarify further. It is time for the first racking!

The exact timing of the first racking is not highly critical; but the longer the wine is left on the fermentation lees, the greater the risk that residual hydrogen sulfide compounds in the lees will be converted into mercaptans. I seldom delay the first racking more than four weeks after fermentation ceases, and I check regularly for off odors or flavors or popped stopper, particularly during the early stages of bulk aging. The first racking is somewhat of a landmark event because it is your first opportunity to speculate on the wine's ultimate quality. Although it will still be very yeasty and its flavor will not peak until two years or so after bottling, you will get a sense the depth of the flavor and the acid-sugar balance.

The purpose of racking a white wine is to hasten clarification so it can be bottled in approximately six months. With each racking some of the impurities will be left behind, either settled on the bottom or clinging to the glass. As a result, there will be less sediment to go back into suspension when the barometric pressure falls, when the temperature rises or when the carboy gets disturbed. After two or three rackings, the wine should be crystal clear and ready for bottling.

The concern when racking is AIR. Until now, air has not been a factor because the wine has been protected in a carboy and capped with either an air lock or a stopper. It has also been saturated with carbon dioxide, which makes it less sensitive to air. But from now on, air will be your number one enemy. White wines are particularly delicate and suffer from any air contact. Each racking exposes the wine to more air and deprives it of a bit of its potential. This is the reason I always sparge the empty carboy with argon prior to racking — to minimize air contact. You can make good wines without an argon tank. But someone devoted to making the very best wines possible should invest $100 in a small tank of argon. It can be used in many different ways to enhance the quality of your wines and make your job easier in the process. Carbon dioxide could also be used, but argon is better because it is heavier and less readily absorbed by the wine. Nitrogen would be a poor third choice.

The number of rackings is kept to a minimum by combining as many treatments and adjustments as possible at each racking. Add meta, oak beans or chips, fining agents, adjust the acid, adjust the residual sugar, etc., all at the same racking, to the maximum extent possible. In addition to minimizing rackings and sparging the carboys with an inert gas, the rackings should take place as early as possible in the life of the wine. That's because a wine will recover from a racking more quickly when it is very young than when it is a year old, by which time it will be considerably more delicate.

Treatments at first racking

The first racking will involve fining with bentonite, adding a dose of potassium metabisulfite and making an adjustment to total acid if it is outside the desired range. Meta should be added now at the rate of 40-50 ppm and another 40-50 ppm at the third racking, just before bottling. Alternatively, some winemakers add about 25 ppm at each racking, which is also acceptable as long as the number of rackings is limited. The important thing in bulk aging is to maintain 20–30 ppm of free sulfite at all times.

Testing and adjusting acidity

The acid, of course, should have been tested when the grapes were crushed and pressed and a correction made then if it was very far outside the range. Since acidity will normally change somewhat during fermentation, it should be re-tested now. Hopefully, a careful titration will find total acidity to be in the desired range of .55–.70%, and an adjustment will be needed only if you want to move it to the optimum part of the range.

If total acid is less than .55%, calculate the amount of tartaric acid needed to raise total acid to that minimum. When adjusting acid, bear in mind that increasing total acid after fermentation by more than a total of approximately.15%, using an artificial acid, is likely to result in noticeable post-bottling harshness. That's why it is important to adjust any major acid deficiency before fermentation—so you won't have to raise it much after fermentation to reach the .55% minimum. Considerably more acid can be added before fermentation than after without affecting the ultimate quality of a wine. At this juncture, of course, you have to live with whatever you did or did not do before fermentation. If you forgot to adjust the acid before fermentation and it is still low after the first racking, add as much tartaric acid as needed to raise total acid to the .55% minimum. But it would be better not to add more than .15% in an attempt to get closer to .65%. (See chapter 8).

If total acid is more than .70–.75%, it should be lowered now if you are making a dry white table wine. I lean toward calcium carbonate at this early stage of bulk aging. It works with greater precision than potassium carbonate, and sufficient time remains before bottling for it to fully precipitate. (See chapter 9).

In lieu of carbonate, a slight excess of acid can be counterbalanced with a higher level of residual sugar. And whether you are raising acid or lowering it, don't forget that blending is a good way to adjust the acid if you have other wine of the right acidity on hand.

Be aware that getting an accurate acid titration reading right after fermentation can be tricky. The wine is still saturated with carbon dioxide, which forms carbonic acid. Although carbonic acid is a weak acid and will eventually be neutralized, it can produce an artificially high titration reading at this stage. To dispel the carbon dioxide, the specimen should be boiled in a microwave oven for twenty seconds and allowed to cool before doing the titration. It is also good practice to run a second test to confirm the first one and, out of caution, to add only half of the calculated amount of tartaric acid or carbonate. That's because an acid or carbonate can have a greater or lesser effect than the arithmetic says it should. In addition, your calculations or measurements might be off.

Making a bentonite slurry

There are numerous fining agents for clarifying white wines, each having advantages and disadvantages. (See Fining Agents Glossary, p. 55). I almost invariably use bentonite first because it is so benign and so effective. It attracts protein byproducts of fermentation and other positively-charge particles. After fining with bentonite, a wine will be "protein stable," meaning that it will not be subject to microbial spoilage or clouding if stored too warm after bottling.

Making a bentonite slurry is easy if you have an agglomerated or prilled form, such as Vitaben or KWK. Just measure 4 teaspoons into 1½ cups of warm water and let it soak overnight. It will be fully hydrated the next day and sufficient to fine 5 U.S. gallons (19 liters). If you are using regular bentonite, you will need to make a hot slurry. This is done by gradually adding 3 teaspoons to 1½ cups of boiling water. (Don't use wine as it will scorch). Boil it for about 20 minutes, stirring as you go and adding water as necessary to maintain the original volume. After 20 minutes it will be fully hydrated, and you will be ready to proceed with racking.

Basic racking procedure

I like to get everything set up and ready for racking before making the slurry. After making sure the receiving carboys are clean and sparged with argon, I dissolve the tartaric acid or carbonate,

as the case may be, in a little water and add it to the empty carboys. Add 50 parts per million (ppm) of potassium metabusulfite
at this racking. This amounts to17 ml of 10% sulfite solution for 5
U.S. gallons, or ¼ tsp of granular, first dissolved in water.

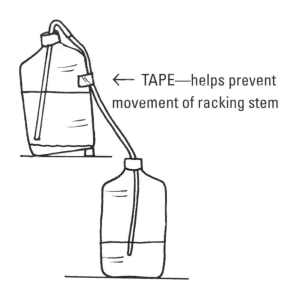

← TAPE—helps prevent
movement of racking stem

ILLUSTRATION C-1: Racking with **no** aeration—for white wines

If the full carboys have not been resting on a bench or counter,
carefully move them to an elevated position. The move will dis-
turb the lees, but the wine will quickly clear again. Gently tip the
carboy and insert a stick under it to create a deep spot. Position
the racking stem at the deepest point in the full carboy, hose attached, and draw up enough wine to fill the hose. Quickly cover
the hose with your thumb and lower it into the empty carboy below. Check the connection between the hose and racking stem to
be sure air is not bubbling in. With white wines the bottom of the
hose should be submerged so as to minimize splashing and aeration. (*Illustration C-1*). With the aid of a funnel, add the bentonite
slurry in small doses at several times while racking. Rock and swirl
the carboy to mix it in or stir it with a dowel. Taping the hose to
the side of the carboy stabilizes the racking stem and minimizes

stirred up lees. Watch the upper carboy and when it gets down to the lees, lift the racking stem to avoid siphoning sediment along with the wine.

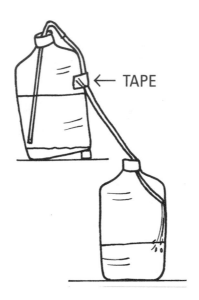

← TAPE

ILLUSTRATION C-2:
Racking with aeration—for first racking of red wines

One caveat if you have small carboys, jugs or bottles full of wine — these containers must be rotated into the main wine at each racking because the wine might not store safely in them until the next racking. Smaller containers should be racked or poured into the new carboy before the wine is racked.

With a little experience you will become quite adept at estimating volumes to get all containers full. In general, fill the largest carboy or container first and use progressively smaller containers for the excess. Top the smallest one with comparable wine or water to displace all air. You could also drop marbles in as a filler. Or displace the air with argon (but not carbon dioxide or nitrogen).

Needless to say, the carboys should be kept full at all times after fermentation is complete. This seems too fundamental to mention, but I have seen many otherwise good wines ruined by long-term aging with too much air space in the carboy. It is even more critical that smaller containers, such as jugs, be kept full and tightly stoppered, as wine cannot be safely kept in them for more than a few weeks under the best of conditions.

Trapped carbon dioxide will continue to effervesce for a few minutes after the racking. Stir it with a dowel to speed up the degassing — you want the trapped gas to escape before bottling. After the bubbles stop, plug the carboy once again with a solid rubber stopper wrapped with sticky plastic wrap and cap it with a fruit jar.

Bentonite precipitates in less than two weeks at room temperature but takes longer at cellar temperture. If you are bulk aging in stainless steel tanks or glass containers that are too large to be moved and cannot heat your room, plan to rack again in three or four weeks. By then, most of it will have precipitated, and the rest will gradually precipitate as the weather warms. Either way is acceptable, but one incidental benefit of racking at room temperature is that the wine will absorb less oxygen during racking than it would if cold.

Fining Agents Glossary

Many different fining agents have been used over the centuries to clarify white and rosé wines. They all carry an electrical charge, positive or negative, and work by attracting impurities of the opposite charge as they precipitate. The more common fining agents described below are all Generally Recognized As Safe (GRAS) by the U.S. Food and Drug Administration, meaning that there is no upper limit on dosage—from a safety point of view. They cause little or no loss in wine quality if used judiciously. The degree of effectiveness depends on unknown variables — what works magically one year might not work so well the next year on the same grapes from the same vineyard. The (+) or (–) below indicates whether the fining agent is positively charged or negatively charged. You will usually need at least one fining agent of each electrical charge in order to achieve total clarity. The information within the brackets [ ] indicates the temperature at which the fining agent is most effective. As a rule, a fining agent should not be pre-mixed with another fining agent or with tannin.

BENTONITE. (–) [Room temp.] 1 tsp = 5.4 g. Bentonite is an excellent fining agent that is both effective and benign. It attracts positively-charged particles in suspension and drags them to the bottom as it precipitates. Seldom can a white wine be fully clarified without using bentonite or some other negatively-charged fining agent. Even if a white wine appears to be clear, it should not be bottled without being fined with bentonite or equivalent. It needs exposure to negatively-charged particles in order to strip out the positively-charged residual proteins and render it protein stable.

My usual dose is 3 teaspoons per 5 U. S. gallons, done at the first racking. See page 52 for making a hot slurry.

AGGLOMERATED BENTONITE. (–) [Room temp.] 1 tsp = 3.7 g. Making a slurry is easier with bentonite that is in agglomerated or prilled form, such as KWK or Vitaben. Add 4 teaspoons to 1½ cups of warm water, let it soak overnight, and it will be fully hydrated the next day — no need to boil and stir. The agglomerated form is also preferable because it compacts more after precipitating, so less wine is sacrificed.

Bentonite is not commonly used on red wines, as it takes out a bit of the color. It has a very high affinity for proteins and will strip out glucolytic enzymes, Scott color enzymes, etc., added at the same time. They should be added after the wine is racked off the bentonite lees.

ISINGLASS. (+) [Cellar temp.] This protein is also effective and benign. I routinely fine with bentonite, followed by isinglass at the second racking. The wine is usually clear and ready to bottle in a few months. I like this combination because bentonite and isinglass function independently of each other and bench trials are not needed to establish an optimum ratio of one to the other, as is the case with kieselsol-gelatin, kieselsol-chitosan and tannin-gelatin. It would be the better practice to do a bench trial for bentonite and a separate bench trial later for isinglass, but I usually use a normal dose of each because they are both so gentle. Some winemakers use isinglass as a polishing agent right before bottling even if the wine is already totally clear because it seems to improve the "mouthfeel" of a white wine.

Isinglass is available in both liquid and granular forms. The liquid form seems to clarify faster. Four ounce bottles of liquid beermaker's isinglass are available at beermaking supply stores, with 1–2 ounces usually being about right for 5 U. S. gallons (19 liters) of essentially clear wine. Note that isinglass will remove residual haze, but it will not clarify a cloudy wine.

GELATIN. (+) [Cellar temp.] 1 tsp = 3 g $\frac{1}{8}$ to $\frac{1}{2}$ g/gal (.03-.13g/L). Like isinglass, gelatin has a protein base and attracts negatively-charged particles. However, it is harsher on the wine and more difficult to work with because it requires tannin to flocculate. If you have too much gelatin relative to tannin, the residual gelatin will stay in suspension. If you have too much tannin, the flavor of the wine could be affected.

Special grades of gelatin are available for winemaking, graded by molecule size, such as 100 bloom, 75 bloom, etc. In my experience, Knox unflavored gelatin seems to work just as well. Granular gelatin is readied for fining by adding it to a small volume of warm water and letting it soak a few hours. Always keep notes on the amounts added. If cloudiness persists, it is usually the result of too much tannin relative to the gelatin, or vice versa. Finding the right ratio is the difficult part of a gelatin-tannin fining regimen. Bench tests should be conducted before fining the whole lot. If you are not set up to run bench trials to determine the right gelatin-to-tannin ratio for the white wine in question, stir in an equal <u>weight</u> of tannin right before or right after the gelatin.

Gelatin can also be used at the rate of $\frac{1}{2}$ to 1 teaspoon per 5 U. S. gallons (19 liters) to soften red wines by removing excess tannin. Don't do frequent finings with gelatin because the full sensory effect of a fining might not be apparent for several weeks.

KIESELSOL. (–) [Cellar temp.] 1 ml per U.S. gallon (.26 ml/L.). Kieselsol enhances the negative charge of suspended particles, making them more negative. As a result, larger particles are formed in the presence of gelatin and precipitation is more complete. Commercial wineries have abandoned tannin in favor of kieselsol as an adjunct for counterfining gelatin because kieselsol-gelatin is a very effective +/– combination and does not run the risk of affecting flavor as tannin does.

If you decide in favor of gelatin-kieselsol at the first racking, skip the bentonite. Dissolve about $\frac{1}{4}$ tsp (~ 1 g) of gelatin in warm

water and stir into 5 U.S. gallons (19 liters). A few hours after racking and adding the gelatin, stir in kieselsol at the rate of 1 ml of
per gallon. Kieselsol is quite heavy and will quickly sink to the
bottom unless the wine is stirred vigorously. A slender wood dowel
is indispensable when fining wines in carboys.

If the wine is not clear in ten days, plan follow it up with a normal dose of bentonite at the next racking. Your chance of success
using only gelatin and kieselsol will, of course, be better if you
run bench trials first. See page 181. Plan to rack about two weeks
after fining.

Some manufacturers recommend adding the kieselsol first for
best results, and others recommend adding the gelatin first.
Winemakers are similarly divided, with some contending that the
sequence results in a subtle difference in flavor.

A gelatin-kieselsol combination is sometimes a good antidote
for the bitter aftertaste that Gewurztraminers and Rieslings tend
to have. Kieselsol has a limited shelf life and should be replaced
when it turns gelatinous. Store it in a cool, unrefrigerated place
and never let it freeze. Numerous brands of 30% kieselsol solution
are marketed, such as Nalco 1072, Klebosol and Neosol.

CHITOSAN, a.k.a. Chitin. (+) [Cellar temp.] Chitosan is a pro-
tein-base fining agent made from the exoskeletons of certain shell-
fish and crustaceans. Used in lieu of gelatin for counterfining
kieselsol, it can produce astounding results in just a few hours,
even with difficult varieties, such as Sauvignon Blanc. If the wine
is not completely clear in a week or two, follow up with bentonite.

Two-part kits of chitosan and kieselsol are marketed by Wine
Art under the brand name of Claro-KC and by L.D. Carlson as
Super Kleer K.C. The kit for white wines has slightly different proportions of chitosan and kieselsol than the kit for red wines. People
allergic to iodine in seafoods need not be concerned about wine
fined with chitosan because the iodine is found in the flesh, not
the shells.

SPARKOLLOID. (+) [Cellar temp.] Up to 1 tsp (1.2 g) per gal.
This proprietary product marketed by Scott Laboratories is used
extensively by commercial wineries prior to filtration as it is extremely effective in removing haze and pectins as well as gentle.
Its biggest drawback for home winemakers is that it will not pre-

cipitate completely by gravity. The only way to eliminate the residual microscopic Sparkolloid haze that otherwise settles out after bottling is by filtration. The post-bottling fluff is harmless but distracting, so I now use Sparkolloid only when other fining agents fall short.

Another drawback of Sparkolloid is that the lees are very fluffy and a disappointing volume of wine is lost. The loss can be reduced somewhat by gently stirring in an ounce or two of isinglass a month after the Sparkolloid has settled.

EGG WHITES. (+) [Cellar temp.] 1 egg white per 15–30 gallons. Egg white is an excellent fining agent for reducing astringency in red wines as well as stabilizing the color. It has been used for centuries and to this day is widely used in France for fining red Burgundies. Separate and discard the yolk. Dissolve a pinch of salt in a cup of warm water — the salt helps liquefy the egg white. Mix in the egg white and whisk to liquefy. One egg white will suffice for up to 30 gallons. In addition to reducing astringency, egg white can be used to increase the brilliance of a finished wine, red or white. Like isinglass, it is not effective to clarify a cloudy white wine. Rack off the lees in about10 days.

POTASSIUM CASEINATE. (+) [Cellar temp.] Consider potassium caseinate as a fining agent if your wine has excess astringency, excess oak, off flavors or colors, or slight oxidation. It is relatively harsh and should be used sparingly. It will coagulate as soon as it is mixed into warm water and will dissolve in a couple hours with occasional stirring. For maximum effectiveness, it should be forced into the wine in a fine stream while racking and be stirred vigorously. A large syringe with a fine tip would be ideal. Very little should be needed — try .14-.26 g/5 U.S. gallons (.007-.014 g/L).

PVPP. [Cellar temp.] Polyvinylpolypyrrolidone is an inert, insoluble plastic powder that can help in removing browning, off flavors and odors, protein haze and excess bitterness. It can also be used to counter the tendency of some blush and rosé wines to turn brown after bottling. If you do not have a pump and filter, use the brand sold as "Polyclar VT" or "Polyclar AT" rather than Polyclar V. The latter will not clear by gravity alone, whereas Polyclar VT or AT might, because the particles are larger. Bench trials are recommended to see if it will be effective — try it at the rate of 2 grams per gallon (1/2 g per liter) as a starting point. Like potassium caseinate, this fining agent is more appropriate for dealing with a specific problem than for general clarification.

Chapter Five

SUBSEQUENT RACKINGS

he bentonite added at the first racking will be fully precipitated in two weeks if the wine was held at room temperature. At cellar temperatures, most of it will be precipitated in three or fours weeks. The purpose of the second racking is to separate the wine from the bentonite lees and treat the wine as follows:

- adjust the acid slightly—if indicated.
- fine with isinglass.
- cold stabilize the wine after racking.
- add oak beans or chips if desired.

Acid adjustment

Do another titration test to check the acid level, first boiling the specimen for twenty seconds to dispel trapped carbon dioxide. Is the acid within the range? Does it taste about right? If it is still too low, add more tartaric acid. How much did you add at the first racking, and how much did it move the reading? Use the amount added at the first racking and result as a guide for this addition.

If the acid is still too high, I would suggest using potassium carbonate at this racking. Calcium carbonate takes a long time to precipitate even at room temperature and would not begin to pre-cipitate during cold stabilization. Potassium carbonate, on the other hand, needs cold stabilization to achieve its full acid-reduction potential.

Acid adjustment at this stage of bulk aging is still a little impre-cise. A little of the natural tartaric acid as well as any tartaric acid that you add will crystallize in salt form and precipitate as potas-sium bitartrate during the cold stabilization that will follow this racking. But the precise amount of acid reduction cannot be pre-dicted will any precision. If you refrigerate and cold stabilize at 27° F (-3° C), the drop might be in the magnitude of .1%; less if you cold stabilize on the back porch. The decrease could be greater than .1% if you added potassium carbonate because a significant part of the chemical effect comes during cold stabilization. On the other hand, I have cold stabilized for two weeks at 27° F and had no crystallization, even after seeding with potassium bitartrate.

See chapter 8 for more details on raising acidity and chapter 9 for lowering it.

Second clarifying agent

This discussion assumes that you used bentonite at the first rack-ing and will fine with isinglass at this racking. Use 1 to 2 ounces of the liquid beermaker's isinglass per 5 U.S. gallons (19 liters). If you are using a granular form of isinglass, such as Biofine, mix it according to instructions.

If you used gelatin-kieselsol or chitosan-kieselsol at the first rack-ing and the wine is still cloudy, give it a normal dose of bentonite at this racking.

Potassium metabisulfite

If you added 50 ppm of meta at the first racking, wait until the next racking to add more. Free sulfite diminishes over time by bonding with aldehydes, oxygen, sugars and other solids, but the 50 ppm added at the first racking will easily tide you over until the next racking. The reason for caution in adding sulfite is that too much total sulfite will tie up some of the esters and diminish flavor and bouquet, even if none of it remains as free sulfite. If you added only 25 ppm at the first racking, add another 10–20 ppm now to replace what is lost through bulk aging and racking. Please be reminded that these sulfite figures pertain to bulk aging in glass or stainless steel. See chapter 14 if you are using oak barrels because free sulfite drops much faster in wood and should be monitored.

Racking procedure

The procedure is the same as the first racking. Sparge your carboys with inert gas if you have a tank. Add everything to the carboy, including the isinglass, and proceed to rack. Stir it with a dowel after racking to help release the trapped carbon dioxide, of which there will still be some. Don't forget to add the small jugs and bottles first!

Cold stabilization

After racking, the wine should be stored cold for three or four weeks while the potassium bitartrate precipitates. An old refrigerator would work well for cold stabilizing but it will hold only one carboy at a time. A walk-in cooler would be more efficient if you have access to one. It helps to stir in 1 tsp of cream of tartar per gallon (1 gram/liter) when the wine is fully chilled to help initiate crystallization. Hold it at a steady 27–30° F (-3 to -1° C) if you can.

Many winemakers, the author included, do not have refrigeration and have to rely on winter temperatures in the garage or back porch to cold stabilize the wine. Depending on your climate, it also works well to store your carboys along the north side of the house, out of direct sunlight. Wine will not freeze as long as its temperature does not fall below 25° F (-4° C). Cap the necks with fruit jars to keep the rain out and check occasionally to be sure the stoppers have not popped out. I experience very few bitartrate crystals after bottling by relying on Mother Nature. The crystals are perfectly harmless anyway, so they don't concern me.

Adding oak beans or chips

If you want to add oak beans, this is a good time to do so. They will become waterlogged and start to sink in a couple of weeks, but by then the isinglass will already have precipitated and will not coat the beans. Five gallons (19 liters) of white wine will safely accommodate 1 – 1½ cups of oak beans, chips, splinters or shavings, as opposed to granular oak or sawdust. Just stuff the beans or chips in; if they produce effervescence, put an air lock back on temporarily.

The oak flavors will be extracted from chips or splinters in about two weeks, but it will take up to ten months to extract all of the flavor out of Stavin's oak beans. Since I do not like pronounced oak, I typically expose 5 U.S. gallons of white wine to one cup of beans for only 30 to 60 days. Depending on how fond you are of oak, you might want to transfer them when you next rack. See chapter 14 for more details on oak additives.

Let the wine cold stabilize for a month or two, or even longer. Some of the bitartrate crystals will re-dissolve if the wine warms up, so do the third racking on a very cold day if possible.

Third racking

The wine should be brilliant by now. One final racking is needed in anticipation of bottling to:

- adjust the acid if necessary.
- boost the level of potassium metabisulfite.
- raise the level of residual sugar slightly. Or not, as desired.

Run another titration test to check the acid level. Does it taste about right? The acid should be close enough by now that you can rely on taste more than the reading. Note that this racking may not even be necessary. If the clarity, acid level and residual sugar are acceptable, you can dissolve ¼ tsp of potassium metabisulfite in 25 ml of water and dispense 1 ml into each 750-ml bottle with a 1-ml pipet. This is 50 ppm. Or dispense .65 ml of your 10% solution, which is also 50 ppm. Then, you can bottle directly out of the carboy and eliminate the third racking. This is not to say that a third racking would reduce the quality of the wine to any noticeable degree, just that you want to minimize racking and air exposure any time you can.

If the acid is still low, raise it to at least .55%, and preferably to .60 – .65%, if you can without violating the rule-of-thumb maximum of .15%. When the acid is getting close to optimum, I often add half the calculated dose and stir in a little more a week later if need be.

If you started out with too much acidity, the prior addition of carbonate will hopefully have lowered it into the .70–.75% range. It is a little late in the game to be using calcium carbonate because it takes so long to precipitate, which would delay bottling. However, it remains an option if the acid still exceeds .75%, as does potassium carbonate. If the acid is still above .75%, I would probably use potassium carbonate to lower it. It is less likely to affect flavor than calcium carbonate. If you use it and choose not to cold stabilize again, the worst outcome would be more bitartrate crystals after bottling. It would be tempting at this point to balance a slight excess of acid (i.e., less than .75%) with a bit of residual sugar.

You might want to add a little table sugar (or honey in the case of Gewurztraminer or Riesling) at this racking to sweeten it to your palate. You presumably ran a Clinitest after the wine fell still and made note of the reading. Although the RS reading should not have changed in the meantime, do a second Clinitest now to confirm the first one.

As discussed in chapter 3, the desired level of residual sugar (RS) depends on your personal preference for the type of wine. Let's assume that you like your white wines fairly dry and that total acid is .65%. A Clinitest indicates that residual sugar is approximately .1%. After bench tests you have decided in favor of a final RS level of .4%. This means that residual sugar will need to be increased by approximately .3%. With 640 ounces of wine in a 5-gallon (U.S.) carboy, you would want to add about 2 ounces of table sugar (640 X .003). Weigh it out, dissolve it in a small volume of hot water, and add it during the third racking.

Renewed fermentation is unlikely because the wine is now fully clarified, and the haze that the yeast cells use as nutrient is gone. The concentration of yeast colonies and dissolved oxygen have dropped well below the threshold required to support yeast multiplication. These factors, plus the fact that the wine is about to be sulfited, combine to make renewed fermentation most unlikely. In the past I have used potassium sorbate, but at only half the recommended rate of 1 gram per gallon. This was out of concern that a full dose would affect the flavor. After learning that half a dose would not be effective to prevent renewed fermentation, I stopped using sorbate altogether and have yet to experience renewed fermentation, even in the case of desert wines. In each instance, however, the wine was fully clarified before the sugar or honey was added.

Additional rackings and fining agents

Occasionally, a wine will not fall brilliantly clear using the bentonite-isinglass regimen. Some winemakers complain about Gewurztraminer, but I have had the most trouble with Sauvignon Blanc. Residual haze leaves you with the decision of whether to live with a little sediment after bottling or whether to venture off into unknown territory by using a third fining agent. Using a third fining agent might set you back in your quest for clarity. If you decide in favor of a third fining agent, bench trials are very important, both to find out whether the third agent will work and also to establish the minimum dose to get maximum benefit. If you don't run bench trials, you will have no way of knowing whether a poor result is due to use of too much or too little of the third agent.

If my wine still contained considerable visible haze after bentonite and isinglass and I was intent on eliminating it, I would probably use Sparkolloid. It is all but guaranteed to produce a wine that is free of visible haze. However, there will inevitably be some microscopic Sparkolloid remaining in suspension that will precipitate as white fluff after bottling, unless you have the capacity to filter. It gets down to a matter of tradeoffs.

Chapter Six

Fermenting Red Table Wines

he procedure for fermenting red grapes is less involved in some respects than for white grapes. Clarification is not the challenge it is with whites, and red wines are not as sensitive to air contact. In this sense, the process is easier for red wines than whites. Note that I did not say it is easier to make a great red wine than white, because I have not found that to be the case.

The general procedure is as follows:

1. The stems are separated and discarded at crushing.
2. The crushed grapes are fermented on the skins in an open container for several days before being pressed. The "cap" of emaciated skins is punched down at least twice daily.
3. When unfermented sugar has dropped to approximately 0° Brix, the wine is pressed and fermentation is completed in a carboy topped with an air lock.
4. Red wines should be fermented warmer than whites — 70-85° F (21–29° C) is the preferred range. A higher fermenting temperature is not mandatory, but more flavor and complexity will be extracted if it is.

A workshop or spare room with temperature control is an ideal place to ferment red wines.

Preparatory

The procedures in chapter 2 for culling out bad fruit, cleanliness and preparation of a yeast starter solution are equally applicable to red grapes. If any of the clusters are hard and raisined, discard them.

Crushing and de-stemming

Since the stems must be separated before fermentation to avoid extreme astringency in the finished wine, it is a great convenience, if not a necessity, to own or have access to a crusher-stemmer. A crusher-stemmer automatically separates the stems while it crushes *(Illustration D)*. Without a crusher-stemmer, at least 90% of the stems

ILLUSTRATION D

will have to be raked out by hand after crushing and the remaining grapes stripped off. This can be done, but it becomes extremely tedious with even as little as 100 pounds. If you don't own a crusher-stemmer, try to borrow or rent one for a few hours.

Improvised de-stemmer—using a milk crate.

After the grapes are crushed and de-stemmed, the mass goes into a primary fermenter, which for most home winemakers will consist of a large plastic garbage can or barrel with a lid. I have several different sizes of the Rubbermaid Brute® containers with lids and find them to be quite satisfactory. The primary fermenter should be filled to no more than 3/4 of capacity to allow room for the cap of grape skins, or *chapeau*, which will rise to the surface as fermentation starts. A normal dose of meta should be added when crushing. Some winemakers omit meta at this stage, reasoning that red grapes have an abundance of tannin, which by itself is a good preservative. However, meta is desirable in my opinion because it kills the malolactic bacteria which might otherwise multiply and establish. There are three strains of malolactic bacteria, two of which are undesirable. If malolactic fermentation is desired, the better procedure is to kill all natural bacteria with meta and add a cultured strain later. In addition, I normally add pectic enzyme at crushing in the belief that it hastens the breakdown of the berry and extraction of color and flavors. One teaspoon of diammonium phosphate per 5 gallons of must will diminish the chance of problems with hydrogen sulfide toward the end of fermentation. It should be added now because it will not help much if added after the problem arises.

Testing sugar, acidity and pH

Fermentable sugar should be a little higher in red grapes than white — 22° to 25° Brix on the hydrometer is ideal. Many fine red wines have been made with higher or lower sugar readings, however. If the sugar Brix is low, add table sugar to raise the Brix to 22-22.5°. If the Brix is above 25.5°, add enough water to lower it to 25° in which case you will want to recheck the acid and raise it to at least .60%.

Be sure to get an accurate titration of total acid. The juice is clear right after crushing, but picks up pigment from the skins soon after fermentation starts, making it difficult to read the endpoint when titrating with phenolphthalein (see *appendix A*). Total acidity should be between .65% and 1.0%, at the time of the crush. It will drop somewhat during fermentation and cold stabilization, probably .05–.10%. If the acidity is close to 1.0%, you will probably want to consider malolactic fermentation as a means of getting it down into the desired range for a finished red wine — .55% to .65%.

Winemakers always want to know the pH of their red wine musts. And for good reason, as it exceeds acidity in importance. The pH, or power hydrogen ion, is a measure of the concentration of hydrogen ions in solution and is basically a measure of the strength of the acidity. The pH of musts should be between 3.2 and 3.6, with the lower figure being more acidic and sour. A pH of 3.5 would be preferable to 3.2 or 3.3 for a finished red wine. Wines with a pH much higher than 3.6 will be unstable and have a shorter shelf life because they are more prone to microbial activity. And wines with a pH below 3.2 will be too sour.

Important as the pH of a red wine may be, it is somewhat academic for the home winemaker, who usually has no control as to when the grapes are picked. And although acid corrections will also affect pH, corrections are normally based on total acid, not pH. So if you do not have access to a pH meter, proceed on the assumption that if the acidity and sugar are in the right range, the pH will be also.

See chapter 8 if your grapes have both high pH and high acid.

Adjusting acidity

The desired acid range for a finished red wine is a little lower than for whites. Total acid in a finished red wine should be approximately .60%–.65%, possibly even as low as .55%, and not more than .70%. Total acidity will, of course, be higher before fermentation.

If total acid of the must is in the range of .65 –1.0%, it will not need to be corrected before fermentation and perhaps not ever. Total acid will normally drop by .05 – .10% or more during fermentation and cold stabilization — this can be expected as a natural part of the process. Malolactic fermentation would lower it by at least .15%, and perhaps by as much as .40%, depending on how much of the total acidity was originally comprised of malic acid. If malolactic fermentation pushes acidity below .55%, it can be raised by adding tartaric acid later.

Similarly, if the must acidity is less than .60%, I would use meta at crushing and plan to press and cool the wine when unfermented sugar has dropped to 0° Brix. Raise the acid to .60% or .65% before fermentation. You can decide after fermentation whether you want to induce malolactic fermentation to get rid of any malic acid flavor. If you know the pH to be high, lower it to 3.50 before fermentation with tartaric acid.

If the acidity of the must is above 1.0%, lower it to that level chemically with calcium carbonate and plan to put it through malolactic fermentation as well. Note that when a must is extremely acidic, the pH is likely to be too low to support MLF. Lowering total acidity to 1.0% before fermentation will probably raise the pH to the minimum level needed to sustain malolactic fermentation, which is about 3.2 in a red wine for most strains of ML bacteria (see chapter 9).

Inoculating and fermenting

When the yeast starter is foamy and active, sprinkle it over the surface of the must without stirring it in. If the must is held at

75- 80° F (24-27° C), fermentation should start in a few hours and will be indicated at first by small, foamy bubbles. After a day, a cap of crushed grapes and skins will be visible. After about two days the cap will rise high, indicating that it is time to add the ML starter and yeast extract if MLF is planned.

Controlling fermentation

There is little that can be done to slow the rate of fermentation of a red must being fermented at higher temperatures. Even a slower yeast, such as Epernay 2, will naturally be very active in the desired temperature range of 70-80° F (21-27° C). No matter what the yeast strain, sugar Brix will drop 10 – 15° within 48 hours after becoming active. You could ferment cooler in order to prolong the fermentation and skin-contact period, but that would be counterproductive as less flavor is extracted at lower temperatures.

For most red wines, it is best to forget about the length of the fermentation period. Keep the room temperature in the 70 – 80° F (21-27° C) range and plan to press when the sugar drops to 0°. At this temperature, due to the heat generated during fermentation, the temperature of the fermenting wine will rise to the desired 90 – 95° F (32-35° C) for a couple of days. This will result in a wine with good structure and complexity and one which will not take years and years to mature. If you are intent on making a "big" wine, see the section on extended maceration in chapter 11.

If your fermenting room is cool, wrap a blanket around the primary fermenter and set the fermenter on a piece of wood to keep it off the cold floor. If this doesn't work, try an electric blanket. It is very important that a red wine ferment warm in order to extract the maximum flavor.

Punching down the cap

The cap has to be punched down at least twice a day during fermentation, i.e., pushed under the surface and covered with fermenting wine. The object of punching down is to prevent aerobic bacteria from developing on the cap and also to promote contact between the wine and skins. Some commercial wineries pump juice from the bottom of the tank and spray it over the cap. The home winemaker has to do it the old fashioned way of punching down.

Almost any flat surface can be used to push it down, such as a stainless steel sauce pan or the bottom of a plastic pail. Care should always be taken not to expose fermenting wines to metals other than stainless steel. Non-resinous wood, plastic and stainless steel are all acceptable. After punching down, the utensils should be removed from the room and washed to avoid attracting fruit flies.

Monitor the temperature during the most vigorous phase, which will occur as the Brix falls from 20° B to 10°. As said, it is desirable that the temperature spike up to 90–95° F (32–35° C). But if it exceeds 100° F (38° C), steps should be taken to lower it. Plastic milk jugs with ice (and a secure cap) are one easy way.

If your grapes had a very high Brix and you are concerned that the level of alcohol might end up too high, the alcohol can be kept slightly lower by fermenting warmer and punching down more frequently and vigorously. This lets more of the alcohol evaporate.

Be alert throughout fermentation for potential problems with hydrogen sulfide. Rotten egg stink requires immediate remedial action. I keep mentioning this unpleasant possibility not because it is so common, but because it is much easier to correct if dealt with promptly (see *appendix B*).

Pressing

When the hydrometer indicates that the unfermented sugar is around 0° B., fermentation will have slowed to nearly a standstill. This will usually be 5 or 6 days after fermentation started. The grapes will be quite emaciated, and the cap will not reform as quickly or rise as high. It's time to press! You could press sooner if the goal is a lighter wine, but it should not be allowed to drop much below 0° Brix because fermentation might stick if it is racked and pressed with too little unfermented sugar remaining. Even at 0° Brix, about 2% sugar remains. The hydrometer is no longer accurate because the high alcohol level has altered the specific density of the liquid.

Dip everything out of the primary fermenter, pour it into the press basket and press in the same manner as white grapes. The hard-pressed portion will have more tannin and be less fruity than the free run, so some winemakers keep the two portions separate and blend them later. Or not, as seems best. It also works well to press lightly and use the remaining must and skins to start fermentation on a concentrate kit. The resulting concentrate wine will be better.

Carboy fermentation

After pressing, the wine goes into clean carboys which are topped with an air lock. Fill the carboys to the top and let the wine ferment to total dryness at approximately 70° F (21° C). Excess volumes can be fermented to dryness in gallon jugs or even in wine bottles if you have an extra small air lock stopper. The small containers will be blended in at the first racking. Continue to monitor for rotten egg smell.

First racking

The remainder of this chapter assumes that malolactic fermentation is not desired; if it was inoculated with MLF starter, skip the meta and refer to chapter 12.

After Clinitest confirms that a red wine is totally dry, it should be racked, sulfited (25-50 ppm) and chilled. Some wines will ferment below .1% on the Clinitest scale and others will stop at .3%, which is the same for all practical purposes as .1%. A red wine should not be left on the lees at higher temperatures any longer than necessary, due to the risk of unwanted side reactions and the tendency of volatile acids to increase. Always lower the temperature as soon as it is dry. If I had no problems with H_2S, I usually let the gross lees settle for about one month and then rack and sulfite. But if I encountered H_2S, I rack and sulfite immediately after Clinitest tells me it is dry and add 0.2 ppm of 1% copper sulfate (page 185). It is always best to lower the temperature as soon as the wine is dry (unless MLF is sought).

Unlike white wines, which suffer from exposure to air, red wines will benefit from a little air contact immediately after fermentation stops. Trickle it down the sides of the carboy at the first racking to aerate it slightly (see *Illustration C-2, page 54*).

For the reason discussed in chapter 2 on white wines, a solid stopper should be substituted for the air lock after the effervescence stops. A stopper that pops out is a sign that microbes are converting the residual sulfur compounds into mercaptans (see *appendix B*).

Subsequent rackings

After a couple of more months, the remainder of the gross lees will have settled, and the wine should be racked again. This time, and at all future rackings, the end of the racking hose should be submerged to minimize aeration *(Illustration C-1, page 53)*. The goal is to give it some exposure to air but not deprive it of air entirely.

Subsequent rackings should take place at increasingly long intervals. Wait three or four months until the third racking, and plan to rack every six months or so thereafter.

The ideal bottling time, assuming that you are bulk aging in glass or stainless steel rather than oak barrels, is in the second year. The fruit level of a dry red table wine that is bottled six or eight months after fermentation will be too high, and it will taste "adolescent" for years to come if deprived of all exposure to air and bottled young. I make this statement based on my own experience after acquiring an argon tank and processing my red table wines the same way I process my white table wines.

Exposing a red table wine to a little air during occasional rackings helps soften the tannins and allows the fruit level diminish to the point where you can appreciate the subtleties and nuances underneath. Bulk aging through the warmer temperatures of summer will also precipitate more of the solids, which means less sediment in the bottle. If you need your carboys for the new crop, at least wait until fall to bottle. But it would be better, if you can, to wait another year to bottle. I add 15 parts per million of potassium metabisulfite at each racking, and if the pH of the wine is high, I treat it with lysozyme early in bulk aging.

Final racking

About a month before bottling, the wine should be racked for the last time. Add 1/4 tsp of meta per 5 gallons (50 ppm). Meta is recommended to rule out malolactic fermentation after bottling and to prolong shelf life. You could also fine with 1/2 to 1 tsp of gelatin per carboy if the wine seems overly tannic and needs to be softened. But give the gelatin a few weeks to settle out before bottling. See chapter 7 for comments on bottling. See *appendix I* for further discussion on the use of meta relative to pH.

Chapter Seven

BOTTLING

 bottling party can be a lot of fun, particularly if livened with samples of prior vintages. But it also involves a great deal of preparation and tedious work. Bottles have to be rinsed and sulfited, wine racked into them and corked and everything cleaned up afterwards. This is undoubtedly the reason so many homemade wines seem to get bottled later rather than sooner!

April or May is a good time to bottle a white wine because it is as clear as you are likely to get it. The temperature will have warmed somewhat by then, so less air will be absorbed during bottling. But if the wine is fully clarified in March and you can get to it, don't wait. There is no benefit in waiting to bottle a white wine once it is clarified.

As discussed in the previous chapter, red wines should be bulk aged through at least one summer before bottling. In fact, if you don't need the carboys for the new crop, a big red wine will be improved by holding it over for a second year before bottling. Two more rackings during the extra year will expose it to a bit more oxygen and help soften the tannins and lower the fruit profile.

New bottles can be purchased at wine supply stores, but the cost mounts quickly if you have much wine. It's a question of how much wine you have and what your time is worth. If you have the time, it's easy to find used bottles at the recycle depot or to get a restaurant or wedding caterer to save them for you. The labels can be soaked and scraped off in a hot solution of soap and trisodium phosphate. Soaps containing a surfactant seem to soften the paper faster. A spray washer attached to an outdoor or laundry sink tap makes rinsing more convenient.

I usually bottle some out of each carboy in 375-ml bottles — these are for early consumption. I like one or two magnums for long-term aging and special occasions — wine truly does age more gracefully in larger bottles. Most of it, of course, goes into 750-ml bottles, which will be the standard for most wine makers.

Corks and closure devices

Closure devices affect the maturation rate of a wine. Crown caps and metal screw caps (but not plastic) do a superior job of retaining the fruit and freshness in a wine, as well as free sulfite. However, the wine will evolve faster with a natural cork. I have always assumed this to be result of the air that gets rammed into the bottle as the cork is inserted and then reacts with the sulfite and tannins.

Another factor in the aging curve of a wine is the method of bulk aging. Wine that is bulk aged in oak barrels picks up minute amounts of oxygen as the barrel is opened, topped up and re-sealed. After a year in oak, it will be farther along the maturation path than the same wine bulked aged in glass or stainless steel. These considerations suggest that while screw caps or crown caps might be fine for a Chardonnay that spent considerable time in an oak barrel, for instance, one would probably not want to bulk age a Cabernet Sauvignon in glass or stainless steel, bottle it young and use metal closure devices. It would take too long to soften and reach its peak. Since red wines are inherently slow to mature, natural corks would seem to be the most logical choice for red wines.

My experience with synthetic and composite materials has been negative. At best, they have not been around long enough to be proved for long-term aging. At worst, they could place your wine in jeopardy. The Australian study[1] found that synthetic corks, such

---

[1]Australian Journal of Grape and Wine Research, Vol. 7, 2001, No. 2. to order: http://www.asvo.com.au.

Steve Foisie of the Boeing Employees Winemaking Club evaluating one of his eastern Washington red wines just prior to bottling.

as SupremeCorq, are inferior at retaining free sulfite. My personal experience, as well as anecdotal feedback, confirms that finding. Free sulfite can drop to zero in less than eighteen months. Altec corks, made of a composite material, retain the free sulfite but taint the wine. The Australian study referenced the taint as trichloroanisole, or TCA, the principal chemical in "corked" wine.

Given these problems and uncertainties, I now use natural corks almost exclusively. I may bottle a few destined for very long-term aging in sparkling cider bottles, filled nearly full and closed with crown caps, but most is protected with natural corks. I know that about 2% will be "corked," but this is an acceptable tradeoff given my experience with alternatives. Someone unwilling to accept a loss of that magnitude might consider "One-plus-One" or "Twin Caps." These closures have a core made of a composite material with a thin "coin" of natural cork glued onto each end. They have been around for several years, are easy to insert and remove, and I have not heard any reports of corked wine. They are competitively priced, too.

Sulfite

No chapter on bottling would be complete without a paragraph or two regarding sulfite. All wines should be bottled with a low level of free sulfite in solution, added shortly before bottling. In most cases, it will be added at the third racking. You can get technical by measuring existing free sulfite and the pH of the wine and calculating how much more sulfite should be added to attain the right level (See page 217-218). If I were a commercial winery, I would certainly be doing that. But as a home winemaker who processes small lots, I usually take the easy way by adding 50 ppm at the third racking and bottle two to four weeks later. Unless the pH is abnormally high, this works well.

Inserting corks

Soaking corks in warm water for a few seconds to lubricate them is optional. If soaked for several minutes, they get spongy and tend to ooze back out of the bottle. It works just as well to insert them dry. Stand the bottles upright for a few hours afterwards to let the air pressure equalize and then store them upside down or on their sides to keep the corks from drying out.

Finishing touches

If you plan to cellar your wine for several years, use of a sealing cap might help keep the cork from drying out. But this is disputed. The relative humidity of the cellar is far more important. Think of a cap and label as an aesthetic touch to something you are rightly proud of! A new Wine Writer® pen or Pilot silver marker will leave an essentially permanent mark on glass. In addition to personal notes on gift bottles, these are handy for marking bottles until you get around to labeling them.

Cellaring

The ideal cellar would have high humidity to keep the corks moist, a constant temperature of 55° F (13° C), and no light or vibrations. I store mine under the house where they are subject only seasonal temperature changes. This works fairly well, even though the temperature gets warmer in the summer than I would like. The white wines are stored at floor level and the red wines higher.

After two months in the bottle, the wine will have recovered from "bottling shock," and you will have your best impression yet of your effort. A white wine with good acid will continue to improve for another two years and a red wine for at least three or four years. It is a gross understatement to say that most home-made wines are drunk too young! A good Cabernet Sauvignon bulk aged in glass does not become drinkable in my scheme of things until it is five years old and continues to improve for many years after that. Even a wine that shows no promise will show surprising improvement after six to twelve months in the bottle. So if you have a questionable batch, don't give up hope; bottle it anyway!

Bottling Glossary

PLASTIC BOTTLING WAND. Many home winemakers use a plastic bottling wand affixed to the end of the racking hose. They can be used with either 5/16" and 3/8" hoses. Wine flows when the valve on the bottom is pushed against the bottle. Top it up slightly so that only about 1/4" of air space will remain after the cork is inserted.

BOTTLE WASHER. This is a faucet sprayer which screws onto an outdoor or laundry sink tap. It is convenient for rinsing a large number of bottles but is not a necessity. I've read that they can damage the water pipes under your house (the abrupt cutoff) but have never experienced that problem.

CORKS. The typical domestic 750 ml bottles uses a no. 9 cork. Some imported bottles have a slightly narrower neck in which the less expensive no. 8's work better. The Australian study indicates that a 44 mm cork will preserve a wine slightly better than a 38 mm cork, but I certainly wouldn't be concerned about the difference unless the wine was destined for at least 10 years of aging. I would avoid corks shorter than 38 mm.

CORKER. If you are on a budget, a hand-held corker is adequate for small quantities. They are slow, difficult to use and scrape off bits of cork as it is forced through the orifice. Bench and floor models are preferable because, in addition to being faster and easier, they compress the entire length of the cork before it gets rammed into the bottle. Be sure to try the model in question if you intend to use composite or synthetic corks, which

Bench model corker

can be difficult to insert. Everyone I have talked to is satisfied with the Ferarri corker, but those with the less expensive Portuguese corker are down right enthusiastic about their investment!

Chapter Eight

RAISING ACIDITY

 s grapes ripen, the sugar content rises and total acid falls. The amount of tartaric acid remains fairly constant throughout the life of the grape; it is other acids—principally malic—that decrease. Grapes grown in hot climates can quickly pass their peak and end up with too little acid and too much sugar. Corrective measures are sometimes needed to bring the acid up to the minimum desired pre-fermentation level of .60 –.65%.

Blending

Blending should be one of the first options to be considered. Natural acids are always to be preferred over manufactured acids, which will eventually taste harsh if added in any significant amount. If high-acid grapes are available, they can be blended with a low acid must. You could even blend in some of last year's high acid wine. Occasionally, I end up with a container of very high acid wine. Rather than lowering the acid chemically, I might hold it for blending with a low-acid wine the next fall. The two could be blended after fermentation is complete. Better yet, blend last year's wine directly into the must at the peak of fermentation (sugar between 20° and 15° B).

Never hesitate to blend any high-acid wine or must into a low-acid one. Unusual blends of varieties can make delightful wines, and it's more fun to experiment than be stuck with a finished wine that is not balanced properly. One caveat in blending is that only wines of sound quality should be used. Never use a wine tainted with odors or off flavors for blending or, contrary to what you might expect, you will usually end up with an even larger batch of equally bad wine. If the wine to be blended has too much acid or suffers from a slight overexposure to oak or sulfite, it will probably be acceptable for blending. But if it suffers from unpleasant organic flavors, such as ethyl acetate or acetaldehyde, even a small quantity will ruin a good wine. So always taste both lots before blending. See chapter 16 for more on blending, including an equation for calculating the ratio of one wine or must to another.

Adding acid

Adding artificial acids is a common method of dealing with acid deficiency, used by commercial wineries as well as home winemakers. It's better to add the acid before fermentation as it will marry better with the natural grape compounds and will be less inclined to precipitate as tartrate salts after bottling. In addition, a must with abnormally low acid is more inclined toward problems during fermentation. If total acid is less than .55%, an acid correction obviously will be needed. Raise it to at least .60% or .65% when you crush because it will drop slightly during fermentation and cold stabilization. Raising it to this level will not result in an overcorrection.

Tartaric acid is normally preferred for raising acidity. It is the dominant and most desirable of the three principal acids. It is also the safest acid to add in that some of it will precipitate as potassium bitartrate during cold stabilization in case you overcorrected. Adding 3.8 g per gallon (1 g per liter) will raise acidity by .1%, but follow-up additions might be needed after precipitation.

Hopefully, acidity will end up in the desired range after fermentation. But if it is much less than .55% after fermentation, it should be raised to that threshold level. Otherwise, the wine will taste "flabby," even if bottled drier, and will have shorter shelf life. I always use tartaric acid in reds, but might add some malic acid to a white must that is very low in acid. Even then, most of the increase should be accomplished with tartaric acid.

Be cautious when adding acid, and never add more than necessary. Raising the acidity of a finished wine by more than .15% with artificial acids is a significant correction which should be exceeded only when necessary. A wine to which more has been added might taste fine initially, but the acid addition will become increasingly harsh and noticeable as the fruit diminishes over time. To avoid overcorrecting, I usually add half the calculated amount initially, taste and test it and add more at the next racking if necessary. It is also good practice to double check your titration reading before correcting.

High pH – high acid grapes

Most of the time, if grapes have a high pH, they will also have low acid and the addition of tartaric acid to raise the acid will bring the pH down to an acceptable level. Sometimes, however, grapes have a high pH and high acid. These grapes are the most difficult to work with because you do not have much freedom to lower the pH by raising the acidity — it's already too high.

It is critical that a high pH-high acid problem be addressed before fermentation. Always take a pH reading immediately after crushing, even if the grower gave you a number. The grower got his reading from a sampling, which is always subject to error. Crushing is the time to start addressing a pH problem because far more acid can be added before fermentation than after. If the pH in the grapes is high and acid is not added until after fermentation, the pH could easily end up so high as to be uncorrectable after fermentation, except at a self-defeating effect on taste. The problem of high pH is magnified further if you wait until after fermentation to address it because the pH tends to go up rather than down during cold stabilization, when the pH of the wine exceeds 3.65. The best solution is to add acid before fermentation.

One rule of thumb is to never start fermentation with the pH above 3.50. If the pH of your must is above 3.50, add enough tartaric acid to lower the pH to 3.50. This might require more tartaric acid than you feel comfortable adding. But remember that unless the must has been pressed and settled, you are testing what is basically free-run juice. The remaining juice to be released from the pulp and skins during fermentation will have even higher pH. Since the pH will normally rise and TA fall slightly during fermentation, malolactic fermentation and clarification, there is a margin of error working in your favor here.

In my opinion, it is better to run the risk of raising total acidity too much before fermentation and having to lower it chemically afterward than to wait and risk having to make a big increase in acid after fermentation just to get the pH in line. A fermenting wine will accommodate a surprising amount of tartaric, compared with a finished wine. The tartaric acid will be much less harsh if given a chance to marry with the cocktail of natural ingredients during fermentation. In addition, it will be less inclined to precipitate as tartrate crystals if added before fermentation.

The pH of red grapes should be monitored closely during the first few days after crushing. The skins contain potassium which gets leached out and raises the pH by an unpredictable but sometimes significant amount. Most of the increase will occur during the first two days after crushing, whether cold soaking or fermenting. If the pH rises unacceptably, consider adding more tartaric.

After fermentation is complete, check total acid, pH and residual sugar. (Remember that at this early point right after fermentation, the sample should be boiled for twenty seconds to dissipate the dissolved carbon dioxide before titrating). Given the nature of the problem, the pH may still be too high. As said, it is harder to deal with after fermentation. Super-chilling the wine down to 25-30° F (-4 to -1° C) is one option. This is an excellent complement to acid addition because some of the tartaric acid will precipitate as potassium bitartrate crystals, which will lower pH. Finished wines with normal alcohol of 12% or more normally will not freeze until the temperature drops below 20° F, (-7° C) and they will turn to slush before actually freezing and breaking the carboy. So 25° F (-4° C) is safe, if monitored. The precipitation process can be hastened by stirring in potassium bitartrate crystals after it has chilled (1 tsp per gal=1gram/liter) — they act as "seeds" to start the crystals growing. The acid level will fall as the tartrate crystals precipitate and the pH will rise, but not by much. The lowered acidity will allow you to add a bit more tartaric acid and cold stabilize again, which will lower the pH further. Each time, some of the potassium combines with the salt anion, which frees up H⁺ ions and thereby lowers the pH.

After raising total acid as much as one dares and successive cold stabilizations, there is little more one can do to correct a finished wine with a high pH. Some winemakers use phosphoric acid rather than tartaric because it lowers the pH relatively faster than it raises the total acid. However, phosphoric acid seems to leave a peculiar flavor if used in any significant amount. It also affects the aesthetic quality of the wine by reducing the body and making it "thinner."

Although it will not lower the pH of a wine, lysozyme will enhance the effectiveness of sulfite by killing potentially troublesome bacteria. Since it does not affect flavor, I routinely add 1 gram per gallon to high pH wines early in bulk aging.

Don't despair if you are forced to accept a higher pH than hoped. A wine with high pH will have a somewhat shorter shelf life, and it will be more prone to spoilage. However, it will last surprisingly well. I once tasted a low acid wine with pH of 4.25, and was surprised that it had not gone off, even after two years in the bottle. It was flabby for lack of acid, but it had not started to spoil. I have also been surprised at the high pH readings on many premium California red wines, some above 3.8. If your wine still has high pH after having been adjusted as much as possible, don't be numbers driven. Bottle it anyway. Use more meta (see *appendix I*), store it as cool as you can, drink it a little sooner and enjoy it a little more while your other wines continue to age.

Acids Glossary

TARTARIC ACID 1 tsp.=4.6 g. 3.8 g./gal. (1g. per liter) raises acidity by +.1%, but some will settle out during cold stabilization as potassium tartrate. It might have to be added a second or even a third time. Tartaric acid is normally the best choice for treating acid-deficient grapes as it is the principal acid found in grapes as well as the most stable. A small quantity of this basic supply should be kept on hand.

MALIC ACID. 3.4 g./gallon (.9g. per liter) raises acidity by +.1%; 1 tsp. = 4.6 g. As grapes ripen, the sugar goes up and acidity goes down; it is principally the malic acid that falls off. Malic acid is acceptable for raising the acidity of white grapes of the fruity variety, such as Riesling, Gewurztraminer and Muscat varieties. It is slightly less sour and a little fresher than tartaric. Tartaric acid will lower the pH of a wine more; so if pH is too high and you want to lower it as much as possible, tartaric acid should be used rather than malic. When in doubt, always use tartaric acid.

Note that only half of the artificial version of malic acid will be converted to lactic acid by malolactic fermentation; the other half remains as malic. This means that if any malic acid was added along the way, a chromatography test will no longer be valid.

(CITRIC ACID). Citric acid is not an essential supply item. It can be safely added only after fermentation and only after malolactic fermentation. It should be avoided in red wine and used most sparingly in white wines. The overwhelming majority of the total acids in a wine consist of tartaric and malic; very little is citric and most wine drinkers would not appreciate a strong citric flavor in a wine. If you think a wine would benefit from a little citric acid, the better and safer choice would be an acid blend.

(ACID BLEND). This is a mixture of tartaric, malic and citric acids which is more commonly used in adjusting acidity in fruit wines. The ratio of acids probably varies somewhat depending on the packager. It is comparable in strength to pure tartaric, but due to the presence of citric acid should be used only in white wines and only after fermentation and MLF are complete. If the acid level needs a significant increase, tartaric acid is again preferable.

(PHOSPHORIC ACID). Some winemakers use phosphoric acid as a way to lower the pH relatively more than raising total acidity. It will do that. However, it affects the wine by decreasing the fruitiness and reducing its body or feel in the mouth. This is something you will have to experiment with and decide for yourself whether the sacrifice in quality is worth the gain in numbers.

Chapter Nine

Lowering Acidity

owering acidity is not as easy as raising it. Ideally, only the malic or citric acid would be lowered and tartaric — the most stable and desirable of the principal acids — would not be affected. Unfortunately, most acid-reduction techniques neutralize all the tartaric acid before affecting any of the malic or citric acid. As a result, care must be taken not to eliminate too much of the tartaric, which would reduce the stability and shelf life of the wine and affect the flavor as well. Here are some options for correcting excess acidity:

Blending

This is again the safest and most conservative choice, if you have low-acid grapes or wine on hand. This will be the exception rather than the rule. So some other technique will normally have to be used.

Amelioration

The addition of water, known as "amelioration," to dilute the acid is a common practice in cool locales where the summers are not hot enough to fully ripen the grapes. One gallon of water added to 5 gallons of must reduces acidity by about 10%, taking into account the ability of an increased volume of liquid to hold more acid. Since it also dilutes the flavor, one–to–five is about as far as amelioration should be pushed.

It is usually a good idea to sweeten the water to about 20° Brix (about 2 pounds per gallon) before adding it. Grapes that are high in acid are probably low in sugar, and sweetening prevents the alcohol level from dropping too low. Although it is generally not a legal practice for commercial wineries in the United States, the practice of adding sugar (known as "chaptalization") is common in many countries where grapes have difficulty ripening.

Amelioration would not be my first choice as a means of lowering acid. But if the acid level of the must were well above the desired maximum of 1.0% (10 g/L), amelioration could be used in combination with some of the following alternatives.

Calcium carbonate

Calcium carbonate ($CaCO_3$), or precipitated chalk, is often used to lower total acid. It does not require cold stabilization to force complete precipitation, as does potassium carbonate. (In fact, it will not precipitate at low temperatures). However, calcium carbonate is more likely to affect the flavor than potassium carbonate and can take many months to precipitate. Due to the latter disadvantage, calcium carbonate is acceptable for reducing acidity in a must or perhaps in a very young wine but should not be used shortly before bottling.

Use calcium carbonate sparingly because it preferentially reduces tartaric acid. Not until all the tartaric acid has been neutralized will it act on the malic or citric acid. Add too much and you run the risk of reducing all the tartaric acid. For this reason, total acid should not be lowered by more than .3% or .4% (3-4 g/L) using either calcium carbonate or potassium carbonate. If acidity exceeds 1.0% (10 g/L), you can draw off one fourth or one third of the must and calculate the amount of calcium carbonate to neutralize all the acid in that portion. Use the formula on page 157 to make sure you will not be overcorrecting. Weigh or measure out about 90-95% of the calculated amount of carbonate, dissolve it in a bit of water, and stir it in. This will reduce all of the tartaric acid and most of the malic and citric acid in the smaller protion. As soon as the foaming is over, mix the treated must back into the main batch. This procedure will allow a greater overall acid correction and still leave ample tartaric acid.

Adding 2.5 g/gal (.66 g/L) will reduce acidity by roughly .1%, but this should be confirmed with bench trials as the effect can vary. It will also raise the pH but by an amount that will vary greatly depending on the chemistry of the must. Since weights per teaspoon of this very fluffy compound vary considerably, it should be weighed rather than measured by volume.

Potassium carbonate

Potassium carbonate (K_2CO_3) reduces acidity by converting tartaric acid to potassium bitartrate which can be precipitated out by chilling the wine for several weeks. Adding 3.8 g/gal (1 g/L) will reduce acidity by about .1%, although its effect cannot be predicted with great precision because you never know how completely it will precipitate. Sometimes it lowers acidity more than expected, apparently by initiating the tartrate precipitation process. So it is better to conduct bench trials before using it. To be conservative, add half of the estimated amount and test the acid level after two or three weeks of cold stabilization. If more is needed, the first addition serves as a guide for the next.

Again, total acid should not be lowered by more than .3–.4% using K_2CO_3 to avoid the possibility of eliminating all the tartaric. And for that same reason, it should not be used in addition to calcium carbonate. Potassium carbonate will raise pH more than calcium carbonate (1 tsp = 6.0 g).

Potassium bicarbonate ($KHCO_3$) is essentially the same as potassium carbonate. Use 3.4 grams per gallon to lower acidity by .1%.

Malolactic fermentation

As discussed in detail in chapter 12, malolactic fermentation is a very effective way to lower acidity and is the most practical choice if a large reduction in acidity is needed. It is unique in that it lowers malic acid without affecting tartaric. The disadvantage of malolactic fermentation is that it reduces the fruitiness in the finished wine. The risk of spoilage is greater at the higher temperatures necessary to sustain the malolactic bacteria.

Cold stabilization

Super chilling a finished wine down to 25-30° F (-4 to -1° C) for an extended period of time will cause some of the potassium bitartrate to precipitate. But unless the grapes had an abnormal level of tartrate salts to begin with, it will reduce overall acidity only slightly, perhaps .05%. It helps to add 1 tsp. per gallon of cream of tartar (from the spice rack) as seed crystals when the wine is completely chilled. Once precipitation starts, the process will gain momentum. An old refrigerator or walk-in cooler is an ideal way to maintain a steady, controlled temperature for the two to three weeks necessary to completely cold stabilize a wine. Storing the wine outside during late fall and early winter is also a satisfactory way to cold stabilize, although some will go back into suspension if the temperature warms. So rack on the coldest day that comes along.

Cold fermenting

Fermenting over an extended period of time at 45-50° F (7-10° C) with a cold-tolerant yeast will cause some of the tartrates to settle out for the same reason as cold stabilization — tartrates are less soluble as the temperature falls and alcohol level rises. Rack the wine off the "mud" during a cold spell and the crystals will be left behind.

Carbonic maceration

Carbonic maceration (chapter 11) is also an effective way to lower total acid. Not all of the malic will disappear, but there will be no lactic acid formed to replace it, as in the case of malolactic fermentation.

Chapter Ten

FERMENTING VARIATIONS – WHITE WINES

he urge to make a better wine runs very high in winemakers! You will soon find yourself contemplating techniques that might be used to improve your work product. Here are some variations in the basic fermentation process which might improve your wine. Although a better wine can never be guaranteed, none of the variations will diminish the quality of your wine.

Soak on the skins

White grapes are often soaked on the skins for a period of time after crushing and sulfiting but before pressing in an attempt to release more of the flavor and varietal characteristic from the skins. Extended soaking for more than a few hours should be done at temperatures below 50° F (10° C). Without access to a walk-in cooler, the home winemaker should be content with an overnight soaking, or perhaps a day or two with some ice jugs suspended in it.

Soaking on the skins is widely believed to increase the varietal characteristic of the grape in the finished wine. Most of my finest white wines were soaked on the skins before fermentation. On the other hand, I have other presoaked wines that picked up an objectionable grassy or herbaceous flavor that I suspect came from the skins. There is no simple answer as to how much skin contact is optimum.

There are so many variables in making wines that one can never be sure of the reason for differing results. Almost any generalization can be debated. And what is true for one year or one vineyard will not hold true for the next. So the following guidelines should be considered with that in mind.

Firstly, if you suspect that the grapes are still coated with sulfur from late or excessive spraying, don't soak them. Press the clusters whole without crushing. If they were crushed and soaked, more sulfur would wash off the skins, end up in the must and be converted to H_2S during fermentation. In addition, if you suspect residual sulfur, add 1 tsp. of D.A.P. per 5 gallons to reduce the tendency to generate hydrogen sulfide.

Grapes that are in poor condition should not be soaked on the skins; skin contact should be minimized. In fact, if the grapes have sunburned and broken skins, low acid, bunchrot or some other defect, consider pressing without first crushing in order to minimize skin contact. And give them the maximum of 120 ppm of sulfite. Pressing without crushing will result in a slightly higher acid level, since the free run juice near the outer surface of the grapes is higher in acid.

The high acid level in under-ripe grapes could be reduced slightly by soaking on the skins and pressing twice. The second pressing will extract more of the juice from the center of the grape which will have slightly lower acidity. Soaking on the skins should also bring out more of the varietal characteristic since the flavors in under-ripe grapes will not yet be fully developed.

Grape type is another consideration. Chardonnay is commonly soaked on the skins as the varietal character is inherently low and can always stand to be enhanced. Sauvignon Blanc is often soaked. But Gewurztraminer, Semillon and the Muscat varieties usually are not. On the other hand, I have made some wonderful Semillons which were soaked on the skins. The rules in this game are made to be broken!

Note that crushed grapes should be kept as cool as possible while soaking. Keep the container out of direct sunlight. If it is particularly warm at the time, drop in a couple of plastic milk jugs of ice (secure cap) and wrap the container with an old sleeping bag or blanket as insulation. Stir the mass occasionally to average the overall temperature. If you are fortunate enough to have access to a walk-in cooler or spare refrigerator, put a layer or two of plastic wrap directly on the crushed grapes to retain the SO_2 and keep oxygen away and let them soak.

Cold ferment

I routinely cold ferment all of my white wines in an unheated garage. Slow fermentation at 50-55° F (10-16° C) will preserve more of the bouquet and fruitiness. Steinberg is an excellent yeast for cold fermenting because it slows as the temperature falls but doesn't stop completely until the temperature gets quite low – below 40° F (4° C). Steinberg was previously used extensively in the commercial fermentation of white wines, but it has lost ground to the more vigorous and faster Epernay 2, presumably so the wineries don't have to tie up their fermenting capacity as long. Epernay 2 is also used for cold fermenting but stops before Steinberg as the temperature is reduced. It tends to leave a little residual sugar, which is often desired in Rieslings and Gewurztraminers. Prise de Mousse is also a good yeast for cold fermenting. My preference is Steinberg because it produces a wine with excellent structure.

Stop fermentation before completion

Rather than letting the wine ferment to dryness and adding sugar back, the better practice is to stop fermentation when unfermented sugar has dropped to the desired level. This is accomplished by fermenting at a cooler temperature and/or using a slower yeast, such as Steinberg or Epernay. It also helps to deprive the yeast of nutrients by racking the juice off the pulp before fermentation and fermenting only the supernatant juice, adding no D.A.P. or yeast food of any type. If these measures are not taken, the wine will quickly ferment right past the desired sugar level before you can intervene.

When Clinitest indicates that unfermented sugar has dropped to the desired level, the slowly fermenting wine should be racked, sulfited and chilled. With nearly dry wines, 50 ppm of sulfite will normally suffice to prevent renewed fermentation if the wine is kept as cold as possible until it has cleared. However, if you have significant residual sugar or if the grapes had significant *botrytis cinerea* (the "noble rot"), the meta dosage should be increased to 100-150 ppm. Stopping fermentation before total dryness is a natural complement to slow, cold fermentation of wines to be left with significant residual sugar, such as Rieslings or Gewurztraminers. Without extra meta, fermentation could restart. Again, keep it well chilled until it has clarified further and been racked again.

Note that stopping fermentation will keep the alcohol level slightly lower. If your grapes had a high sugar content, such that you are concerned about a "hot" wine (i.e., where the alcohol detracts from aesthetics), stopping fermentation at 1% RS, for example, would keep the alcohol lower by about .55%.

Some winemakers routinely stop fermentation whenever they want some residual sugar rather than fermenting them dry and adding back sugar. This is the better technique. The only drawback in racking and sulfiting before complete fermentation is that it takes longer to clarify. The same minor problem will arise if you reserve some original must in the freezer and use it to sweeten after fermentation. For some reason, the wine clears more readily if it is allowed to ferment all the way to dryness and the gross lees allowed to settle before being racked. But this is not a major problem as it will usually clear anyway, given more time.

Ferment the free-run must separately

Wineries and home winemakers alike often ferment the free run juice separately. As the crushed grapes are poured into the press basket, about half of the total juice will flow through before pressing even begins. This is known as the "free run" must and will usually have slightly higher sugar and slightly higher acid than the pressed juice. The free-run must is widely believed to produce a higher quality white wine.

Pour the crushed grapes into the press basket and catch the free run juice as it drains. Add the usual 50 ppm of meta and transfer the must to carboys to let the pulp settle out. Rack the clear juice off the pulp the next morning. Add some yeast food if a dry wine is the goal, because the discarded pulp contains a lot of nutrients. Adding D.A.P., yeast extract or a balanced yeast food along with the yeast starter will encourage fermentation to complete dryness.

With 200 pounds of grapes, you will have approximately 6 gallons of free run juice, which will be enough to fill a carboy after fermentation is complete. Ferment 3 gallons in one carboy and 3 gallons in another and combine them near the end of fermentation. Ferment the hard-pressed juice separately in a third container. If you do not detect enough difference between the free run wine and the pressed, the two can be blended after completion of fermentation. Note, however, that the difference between the two lots might not become apparent for six months or a year, when they are more delicate.

Although the free-run must is widely believed to produce a superior wine, I have not been able to confirm that. I am, however, a firm believer in settling a must and discarding the pulp.

I once fermented 4 gallons of pure pulp from three different varieties of white grapes. The pulp compacted during fermentation and the resulting 3 gallons of wine was initially very clean and delicate, although light bodied. After a year in the bottle, it had lost all its fruit and seemed quite acidic and alcoholic, even though both were lower than the wine from the clear juice. This gives credibility to the practice of commercial wineries of settling and discarding the pulp and fermenting only the clear juice.

Pre-fine with bentonite

Pre-fining with bentonite will remove protein impurities and solids from a must and is something to consider for grapes having too much *botrytis*. Since the bentonite will remove nitrogen, it will make it easier to stop fermentation with a higher level of residual sugar remaining, where that is desired. Pre-fining might also help reduce the flavor level of *labruscas.*

Crush, sulfite and press as usual. Then make a bentonite slurry (1 tsp. per gallon) and stir it in while racking. Let it settle overnight and rack the supernatant juice off the pulp and finings the next morning. The disadvantage of pre-fining is that it will affect the complexity of the finished wine.

Ferment the dregs and leftovers - *Sur Lie*

Aging *sur lie* is a recommended way to enhance the mouth feel of a white wine and impart a slight yeasty flavor. Rack off the gross lees about three weeks after fermentation stops. Then stir up the lees with a dowel once a week for several months. Sulfite is not needed because the yeast lees are an excellent antioxidant. Then proceed with your normal fining and clarification regimen.

You can also combine the leftovers from several different fermentations together to make what I very loosely label as a "cuvée." Keep adding the lees, sediment, yeast "mud" and excess volumes of the different varieties as you rack and consolidate carboys. Add the mud, even if it's all that remains from a racking! You might end up with 50% solids. It doesn't look very appealing, but after a few months on the lees with an occasional stirring, the wine will acquire a delicious, yeasty flavor. Make sure each container is fully topped up when the wine finishes fermenting, or keep the carboy flooded with argon. Keep it cool and stir up the lees occasionally with a heavy dowel. On more than one occasion, my *cuvée* was my best white wine of the year! A venture of this nature obviously assumes you encountered no H_2S during fermentation.

Malolactic fermentation

It is more difficult to induce malolactic fermentation in white wines, and it diminishes the fruitiness. But MLF adds a unique, "buttery" flavor and is a very good way to lower acidity. See chapter 12— Malolactic Fermentation.

Glucolytic enzyme

Gistbrocades AR 2000 enhances the bouquet of aromatic wines, such as Gewurztraminer, Riesling, and the Muscat varieties. The recommended dosage is 1 to 5 grams per hectoliter (100 liters, or 26.4 U.S. gallons), with 2 grams being my personal standard. Dissolve 1 gram (1/4 tsp.) of the enzyme in 25 ml of water. This will inoculate 26 gallons at the rate of 1 gram per HL or 13 gallons at the rate of 2 grams. AR 2000 can be used late in fermentation or during bulk aging and should be allowed to run its course before bottling.

First do bench trials. Test at the rates of 1 gram per HL, 2 grams per HL and 3 grams per HL. With gallon jugs, this means using 1 ml per gallon, 2 ml per gallon, etc. With 750 ml bottles as containers, it takes only 0.2 ml and just half that for 375 ml bottles. To make measuring more accurate for small bottles, dissolve 1 gram in 100 ml of water and use 0.8 ml per 750 ml bottle or 0.4 ml per 375 ml bottle for the rate of 1 gram per HL. You will need a 1 ml pipet to make these measurements. Store your samples at room temperature for a month using an air lock. (It would take longer at cellar temperatures to get the full effect). Then make your sensory evaluations. Note that bentonite or Sparkolloid added shortly before or after this enzyme will strip the enzyme out before it has done its job. If you want to blend a treated wine with an untreated wine, the treated wine should be fined with bentonite before blending. Otherwise, enzyme activity will resume after blending.

This product will result in a very floral wine that is ready for consumption sooner. However, the bottle aging curve is changed. Wines treated with AR 2000 seem to peak much sooner and do not continue evolving over the years as do high quality untreated wines.

Oak during fermentation

A barrel fermented white wine will have a different character than one which is barrel aged. Use three ounces of oak beans per carboy or a small stave during primary fermentation. This is the functional equivalent of barrel fermentation.

Ice wine

The term "ice wine" does not have a universal definition, but in some wine regions the term is restricted by law to wines made from grapes that were left to hang into the winter and harvested at sub-zero temperatures — at least 19° F (-7° C), and preferably 9-14° F (-10 to -13° C). By then the berries have lost a good deal of their original water content, the yield is greatly reduced, and the flavors are dramatically intensified. The grapes are picked and crushed while frozen solid, often at night. The water freezes but the sugar does not, so the volume is further reduced at these low temperatures. The ice shards can be strained out to reduce the water content and intensify the flavor further. The picking process is very labor intensive and the yield low, all of which combine to make ice wine exceedingly expensive.

Historically, ice wine has come from Germany and Austria, but Ontario's Niagara Peninsula is probably the largest producer today. British Columbia is also a producer. Vidal and Riesling are the most common varieties used. The appellation regulations in these areas forbid the artificial freezing of grapes. To make true ice wine, all you have to do is go out some dark December night when it is appropriately cold and pick only those berries that are shriveled and dried out but not rotten. After a few hours, you might have enough grapes to make a gallon of wine! This assumes that you have access to grapes that have been left to hang.

If this approach looks too daunting, get late harvest grapes and try making a "false ice wine." Freeze them in your freezer or a locker plant, press them while still frozen and strain out the ice shards. As always, the quality of the grapes remains the paramount consideration, not whether they were frozen by Mother Nature and picked at night.

Rather than working with frozen grapes, I usually crush, press and then freeze the must in small containers or large Ziploc bags. It might take two or three days to freeze. Thaw the bags one at a time in a plastic or stainless steel colander set atop a plastic pail or vitreous crock. After a few hours most of the sugar and juice will have dripped out, and a porous ice core will remain. Discard the ice core before it melts and dilutes the must; the sooner you toss the ice core, the higher the Brix will be. Repeat this tedious process with the remaining bags of frozen juice. [Tip: If you like to

Colander with thawing ice core.

ferment concentrates, you will get a superior wine by using the ice cores rather than water to hydrate the concentrate!]

Monitor the Brix of your must as the ice cores thaw. To make a sweet desert wine you want to start fermentation with sugar of approximately 34° Brix. If the Brix is higher, let more of the ice cores thaw. If you want to make a drier, Alsatian style of Gewurztraminer or Riesling, let even more of the ice core melt and start fermentation at 28° Brix.

Reducing the volume will increase the total acidity of the must, so the final wine may have to be balanced with higher residual sugar. Reserve about 10% of the must volume before fermenting, hold it in the freezer and use it after fermentation for sweetening the final wine. Reserved must is better than adding sugar or honey because it gives more flavor, although it is also suspected of adding a bitter aftertaste that table sugar does not. Epernay 2 yeast is commonly used for ice wine because it is not very vigorous and tends to stop fermenting with a few points of residual sugar remaining, which is what you want. Steinberg is also good — it is a strain that is difficult to stop by lowering the temperature, but it is sensitive to sulfite.

Vidal, Riesling, and Gewurztraminer all lend themselves nicely to this technique, as does late harvest Sauvignon Blanc. Late harvest grapes are preferable to early season grapes as they will already have a higher sugar level, more flavor, and hopefully some *botrytis cinerea*.

Fermentation Notes – Ice Wine

DAY 1 – 5 gal. bucket of Gewurztraminer arrives by UPS, fully thawed, but cold. Took readings (21.8° B., 0.7% TA; label says: 20.9° B., 0.8% TA, 3.15 pH, and 15 ppm sulfite). Diverted 3 qts. to restart a different batch of Gewurz. that is stuck and immediately refroze the rest in bowls and 1-gallon Ziploc bags. Held back 1 cup to make a yeast starter solution (Epernay 2/ Cotes de Blanc). The must took about 36 hours to completely freeze.

DAY 3 – Rigged a plastic colander atop the 6-gal. bucket. Put a chunk of frozen must in the colander and the fermenting yeast starter solution in the bottom of the bucket. The juice drips into the yeast starter as it thaws. About 6-8 hrs. later (depending on temperature), the goodies had dripped out and only the ice core remained. Discarded the ice core.

Repeated the thawing procedure until all the frozen must containers were thawed, discarding the ice cores. The goal is a concentrated Gewurztraminer juice with more intense flavors. With less volume, both Brix and total acid will be higher. The higher acid will be balanced with a higher level of residual sugar.

DAY 5 – The juice is all thawed, except that one is held back for sweetening after fermentation. Transferred the rest of the thawed juice to a small carboy and topped with an airlock. Freezing, thawing and discarding the ice core raised the Brix by about 5° B; it also raised the total acid; did not take measurements. Had to bring it inside to get fermentation started. Could have raised the Brix more by discarding the ice cores sooner.

Thereafter, followed the procedure for making any white wine. After clarification it needed to be sweetened to balance the elevated acid level.

Sweetening with reserve must without causing renewed fermentation. This is not as tricky as it would seem, but it is imperative that the wine be totally clarified before adding the reserve must. The haze in white wines is a nutrient for yeast and has to be removed. I let the wine ferment to "dryness" and gave it about a month to clarify. By then, most of the gross lees had settled out. Racked and sulfited (30 ppm) after one month. Let it clarify for two more months, by which time it was very clear. Fined with bentonite—slurry of 1 tsp per 5 gal. Racked 3 or 4 weeks later, adding the reserve must and 50 ppm sulfite. You could also add potassium sorbate if you feel it is needed. Later added AR 2000 glucolytic enzyme to enhance the bouquet—at the rate of 2 g per 25 gal., and still later, bottled.

Chapter Eleven

FERMENTING VARIATIONS — RED WINES

here are fewer fermenting alternatives for red wines than whites. Red wines are typically fermented to complete dryness and bottled with no residual sugar. The principal variable is the length of time the grapes are in contact with the skins and seeds, which can greatly affect the outcome. Malolactic fermentation is covered separately in chapter 12.

Cold Soaking—Early Pressing

Red grapes can be soaked on the skins for several days prior to fermentation. This deepens the color of the wine and allows for earlier pressing, before the harsher, alcohol-soluble tannins are extracted. It also gives the berries more time to disintegrate before pressing. Cold soaking is commonly done in conjunction with early pressing.

Here is how one might cold soak and ferment a batch of Pinot Noir grapes. Crush and de-stem as usual. Sulfite is optional. Pectic enzyme could be used to good advantage. Lay some strips of plastic wrap over the surface and chill it to 45-50° F (7-10°C) for about four days. Then let the temperature gradually rise and sprinkle the yeast starter over the surface of the must. After fermentation has started to the point where there is a cap, start punching down. You could at this point draw out some fermenting juice (no skins) and ferment it separately into a rosé. With all the skins and less liquid, the remaining wine will have slightly more body. Unless the total acid is abnormally low, you will want to put the wine through malolactic fermentation. Inoculate now, right after the rosé is withdrawn.

The must temperature during most of the fermentation time should be in the 70-80° F (21-27° C) range, but it is desirable to let the temperature spike up to 85 -90° F (29-32° C) for a day or two in order to extract some of the phenols that would otherwise be left behind. This elevated temperature tends to occur naturally during the vigorous phase of fermentation — i.e., when the unfermented sugar level is dropping from 20° B. down to 10° B. Punch down as usual during fermentation.

Early pressing goes hand in hand with cold soaking. If the goal is to maximize the water-soluble tannins and minimize the alcohol-soluble tannins, it follows that you want to press early. You can press any time after the Brix has dropped below 10° and should press no later than 0° B., (i.e., after about four days of active fermentation). Maintain a 70-75° F (21-24° C) temperature after pressing to carry malolactic fermentation through to completion. Cold soaking and early pressing will produce a wine that has a high fruit profile (because the tannins have been minimized) and which will age much faster but presumably have a shorter shelf life.

Although access to a walk-in cooler is a great convenience for cold soaking, it is not a necessity. Get a good supply of plastic milk jugs (with lids) and freeze them nearly full. Put two or three in the primary fermenter to chill the must and keep two or three in the freezer. Keep the fermenter in the coolest place available, drop in fresh jugs every day, refreeze the thawed ones and the must will be kept cold. It helps to wrap the fermenter with an old blanket or sleeping bag as insulation. Rather than jugs, you could use blocks of ice in large garbage bags (double-bagged, just in case). The must should be stirred daily and the temperature monitored.

Extended maceration

Extended maceration is the opposite of short skin contact. The idea is to leave the still wine in contact with the skins and seeds after fermentation is complete in order to maximize the extraction of tannins and phenols. Commercial wineries working with high quality grapes and wanting to extract the maximum flavor often do this with part of the crop and use it for blending. The still wine is held in airtight vats for a period of time ranging from several days to several weeks. The air space is kept flooded with an inert gas to prevent exposure to air and acetification. Note that the color will not get deeper during extended maceration; in fact at some point in time the skins will start reabsorbing the pigments and the wine will lose color. But extraction of tannin and phenols will increase as they are more soluble in alcohol than water. Interestingly, the added complexity comes from the seeds, not the skins.

The secret in extended maceration is to catch the change in tannins at just the right point in time and press then. The wine will fall still after 12 to 13 days of fermentation, and several days later the cap will sink. The vintner tastes the wine on a daily basis, awaiting a change in the chemical makeup up in the tannin. One day, the wine will taste dramatically softer, as though it has aged much longer than it really has. The wine is quickly pressed within a day or two. If pressing is delayed, the wine quickly becomes more tannic. So pressing takes place during this short window of opportunity.

Few home winemakers will own the ideal equipment for extended maceration (a stainless steel primary fermenter with a floating lid or Graf poly tank and a tank of argon or carbon dioxide) because this equipment is expensive. Nevertheless, it is possible to do extended maceration using a Rubbermaid Brute® or comparable primary fermenter with a lid. The most important thing is to protect the wine from air after fermentation ceases and CO_2 is no longer being produced. Here is how I have successfully done extended maceration using an ordinary fermenter.

Crush, ferment and punch down as usual for red grapes. Once the sugar level has dropped to approximately 0° B. on the hydrometer, start laying strips of plastic wrap directly on top of the diminishing cap. This will trap the slight CO_2 that is still being produced and hold it next to the wine; it also acts as a barrier against air. Maintain an elevated temperature of 75-80° F (24-27° C). (The cap will sink if the temperature is allowed to drop). There will be a little effervescence as the remaining sugar ferments plus a little from malolactic fermentation — this helps maintain a cap. Continue punching down, but once a day will suffice from now on. Replace the plastic wrap and fermenter lid each time. The wine should be tasted every day from this point forward. It might get harsher at first, but will mellow dramatically one day soon. Time to press!

After 12 or 13 days with the temperature being held at 75-80° F (24-27° C), fermentation will be complete. Completion should be confirmed with Clinitest, not a hydrometer. Malolactic fermentation might also be complete, particularly if you inoculated right after fermentation started. Run a chromatography test now if you are curious (see *appendix A*). If it is complete, you will want to sulfite at the time of pressing and lower the temperature. If you feel uneasy by the fact that no carbon dioxide is being produced, you can keep the air space filled with an inert gas by using your tank if you have one or by drilling a 3/8″ hole in the lid and using a CO_2 pot (see *appendix C*). Or use argon, if you have it.

Some home winemakers (and wineries as well) like to wait until the cap has sunk before pressing. This will occur when MLF is complete and when most of the trapped carbon dioxide has escaped. Or when the temperature falls. However, by waiting until the cap sinks, you might miss the window of opportunity, when the tannin softens. The better practice is to press by taste.

In most cases the softening will be so dramatic as to leave no doubt. A wine that one day is totally undrinkable will be glorious beyond description the next day. It will be mellow and have overwhelming fruit and flavor. This is the time to press. Pressing could wait a few more days without permanently damage to the wine; but the longer you wait, the longer it will take to age. What you want to avoid is extended skin contact long after the softening.

Note that although the softening will normally occur between two and three weeks after crushing, it is somewhat temperature dependent and could take longer if the temperature was less than 75° F (24° C).

Make a rosé

Good rosés are not appreciated in the United States to the extent that a winery can afford to divert quality red grapes, such as Cabernet Sauvignon, Merlot or Zinfandel. This is not a consideration for the home winemaker because revenue is not a consideration. In fact, by drawing off part of a red grape must that has fermented on the skins for only a short while, you might end up with the best of both worlds — a delicious rosé and a highly-extracted red wine of better quality than it otherwise would be.

Crush and de-stem the grapes as though a red table wine were to be made, using 50 ppm of meta to discourage malolactic fermentation, which is not desirable in rosés. Prepare a yeast starter solution and inoculate the must as usual. After it has fermented on the skins for a few hours or perhaps a day, dip out part of the must (no skins) and transfer it to a carboy to ferment to dryness.

The question of when the rosé portion should be drawn off is a decision that is largely personal to your goal. The longer it is left to ferment on the skins, of course, the more color and complexity it will acquire. And the longer it will take to mature. Check the color frequently, and when it looks right to you, make the transfer. Let it get a little darker than you think you would like because the color will lighten as the solids precipitate and the wine clears.

Continue fermenting the rosé portion separately, in a carboy, as though it were a white wine. The procedure for fermenting and clarifying white wines should be followed from this point forward. Since most people expect a touch of sweetness in a rosé, residual sugar should probably be around 1%, possibly higher. After the wine is still and the gross lees have settled, add some cane or beet sugar back to raise residual sugar to the desired level. Or you could stop fermentation at the desired point by racking, sulfiting and chilling. See page 95.

Continue fermenting the rest of the original must as you would for a normal red table wine. Punch the cap down twice daily and press when the unfermented sugar reaches 0° Brix. Since all of the skins are concentrated in a smaller volume of wine, the extraction of phenols and intensity of flavors should be higher. If you want malolactic fermentation in this portion, add the starter right after the rosé portion is removed.

The entire crushing could be fermented into a rosé. Crush, de-stem, sulfite and ferment the entire crushing on the skins for a day or two until the desired color is attained. Then press and finish in carboys as you would a white wine.

In cold, wet years when red grapes don't ripen and will not make a premium dry red table wine due to high acidity, it will be easier to get desirable red *vinifera* grapes such as Cabernet Sauvignon. The higher acidity can be countered with higher re-sidual sugar.

The pinkness in rosés sometimes turns brown after bottling, diminishing the wine's appeal, but not ruining it. To minimize this possibility, you could do two things: 1) Add no meta until after fermentation; and 2) fine with Polyclar VT. See page 59.

Carbonic maceration

Carbonic maceration is a good way to lower total acidity and end up with a unique red wine in the process. The grapes are not even crushed; they are placed in an air-free atmosphere at 80° to 90° for two or three weeks. It is the natural enzymes within the berry, not yeast, that convert the sugar to alcohol. The resulting wine is relatively low in tannin, very dark in color and has an unusual fruity quality akin to volatile acidity or malic acid that you will either like or dislike.

Carbonic maceration is often used to enhance wine made from under-ripe, high-acid grapes of lesser quality. It can be used with premium fruit as well but seems to capture less of the fruit flavor than conventional fermentation. Regardless of the fruit, the chal-lenge is keeping air out until the enzyme process starts and begins generating its own CO_2, as the grapes would spoil quickly if ex-posed to air at the higher temperatures necessary to initiate the enzyme process.

The ideal procedure would consist of completely filling an air-tight container with whole clusters of red grapes, displacing the air with CO_2, sealing it against air penetration and pressing after about three weeks at 85° F (29° C). A stainless steel vat with float-ing lid would be an ideal piece of equipment for carbonic macera-tion, as would a Graf poly container, since both are air tight and have an air lock. But let's assume you have nothing to ferment it in other than a Rubbermaid Brute® primary fermenter and lid and want to try carbonic maceration. Here's one way it can be done.

As soon as the grapes arrive, crush and de-stem about 10% of the batch. Initiate fermentation in this portion with a dependable wine yeast, such as Prise de Mousse, before adding the grape clusters. The purpose of fermenting this small batch of ordinary red grape must is to generate sufficient CO_2 to displace the air in the container and protect the grapes until the enzyme process starts a few days later.

Once fermentation has started in this small batch, dump it into the container. Now add the remaining 90%, which will be whole clusters on the stems. Ideally, the container would be full to the top. Put the lid in place and tape it with many layers of duct tape. You probably will not be able to totally seal the container, so tape it as best you can.

To be on the safe side, I would also recommend drilling a $3/8$ inch hole in the lid and inserting a straight-stem air lock so that CO_2 gas can be transferred from a carboy of fermenting wine or sugar water (see *appendix C*). Since you will not know for sure how fast the sugar is being converted to alcohol or when it slows down or stops, plan to press two to three weeks after the container is sealed. If you cannot keep the room temperature at 85° F (29° C), wrap the container with an electric blanket set on high.

When the container is opened in two or three weeks, the grapes will look almost the same as the day they were added. But they will have lost all their structure and firmness and will collapse with the slightest pressure. There will be a considerable amount of wine accumulated at the bottom of the container, consisting of the original fermented portion plus additional juice that dripped out of the clusters during maceration. This can be racked out before pressing and kept separate as it has less carbonic flavor than the wine remaining in the clusters.

The pressed and "free-run" portions will both still have several points of unfermented sugar and should be fermented to dryness under air lock. The two lots can be combined at pressing. Or they can be fermented to dryness separately and blended later, or not, as appeals to you. The pressed portion will have more carbonic flavor than the other.

Here is a variation that can be used to add a touch of the carbonic flavor to a traditional fermentation of Pinot Noir, for example. Set aside a small part of the grape clusters before crushing and de-stemming, at most 10%. After the main portion has been crushed and de-stemmed, add the whole clusters back and ferment normally in an open primary fermenter but at 80-85° F (27-29° C), punch down, etc. The carbonic process will take place within the whole berries and become part of the overall wine when everything is pressed. But the carbonic quality will be less pronounced.

Pinot Noir and Gamay grapes are the classic grapes for carbonic maceration. In my opinion the flavor of these grape types is highly compatible with the carbonic flavor that results. Since these two varieties are low in tannin, it is better to use whole clusters with stems; the resulting wine will still be low in tannin. If you are using red grapes which have more tannin, such as Cabernet Sauvignon or Zinfandel, the grapes could be stripped off the stems to keep the tannin level lower. Even with Cabernet Sauvignon, I have found the tannin level to be high, but not ruinously so as a result of using whole clusters.

Chapter Twelve

MALOLACTIC FERMENTATION

alolactic fermentation (MLF) imparts a unique flavor which is particularly noticeable in white wines, takes some of the sharpness off the acid as it is perceived around the edge of the tongue, and "rounds out" a wine. MLF is commonly sought in dry red table wines, provided must acidity is not too low to start with. It is also used for some dry white wines, such as Chardonnay, Sauvignon Blanc, Pinot Gris and sometimes Semillon, but is generally avoided for fruity white wines, such as Riesling, Gewurztraminer, Muscats and Chenin Blanc. The diacetyl produced by malolactic bacteria is the principal source of the "buttery" quality in Chardonnays.

Malolactic bacteria break down the malic acid into lactic acid, producing water and carbon dioxide in the process. Since lactic acid is only half as acidic as malic acid, total acidity is lowered by half the amount of malic acid converted. For example, if the original malic acid content happened to be .4% and all were converted to lactic, total acidity would drop by .2%. MLF is the only practical way for the home winemaker to selectively reduce malic acid without first neutralizing all of the tartaric acid, which is the desirable acid.

Malolactic bacteria occur naturally in the air and on the grapes. If potassium metabisulfite is omitted, the malolactic bacteria might multiply to the point where they will do their job. However it might not happen until the following spring or summer, if at all, and the wrong strain might develop. Since two of the three strains of malolactic bacteria are undesirable, the better practice is to kill all malolactic bacteria by sulfiting at crushing and inoculating later with a pure strain of the desired bacteria, *leuconostoc oenos*. The outcome is both faster and more certain this way.

Note that potassium sorbate should not be used if you seek malolactic fermentation because it is a nutrient to the bacteria which results in an objectionable "geranium" flavor.

Adverse conditions

Malolactic bacteria are finicky critters. They thrive only under certain conditions and even then, nothing is guaranteed. Here are the conditions in which they struggle. If you want MLF, do your best to *avoid* these conditions:

HIGH ALCOHOL. Malolactic bacteria are not very tolerant of high alcohol levels, which is why it is more difficult to initiate MLF in still wines. If your grapes have high sugar and you want malolactic fermentation, inoculate early in fermentation, before much sugar has been converted to alcohol.

HIGH SULFITE. Malolactic bacteria are much more sensitive to sulfite than yeast are. Even a modest level of 25 ppm of free sulfite is likely to kill malolactic bacteria. It is best in my opinion to use $^1/_4$ tsp. per 5 gallons (= 50 ppm) at the time of the crush. This kills all natural malolactic bacteria, including the bad strains. If you want MLF, inoculate later with a cultured strain. Note that total sulfite in excess of 100 ppm is also likely to inhibit MLF, even if none of it is in free state.

LOW TEMPERATURES. Most strains of *leuconostoc oenos* are barely active at 65° F (18° C). The "OSU" strain will work at lower temperatures, but all strains are more active in the desired temperature range of 75-80° F (24-27° C).

LOW pH. If your grapes have high acid, the pH might be too low to cultivate malolactic bacteria. The traditional malolactic bacteria will work in red wines having a pH of 3.3 or higher and in white wines having a pH of 3.1 or higher. If you do not know the pH of the must, but know that total acid is high and want mal-olactic fermentation to reduce acidity, use calcium carbonate to lower the total acidity to 1.0% before adding the malolactic starter.

Malolactic bacteria might tolerate one adverse condition, but not two or three. It is quite easy to avoid MLF — just use sulfite, keep the temperature down, and clarify the wine before allowing the temperature to rise, and it would be most unusual to experi-ence any MLF.

It's much more complicated if you want MLF. Great care must be taken to make the conditions as ideal as possible before adding the starter — no free SO_2, temperature at 75 -80° F (24-27° C) and proper acidity and pH. It also helps to use yeast extract as a nutri-ent at the rate of 1/2 g/gal and to stir up the lees and nutrients with a slender dowel once or twice a week. Note that although yeast love diammonium phosphate, malolactic bacteria are indif-ferent to it.

When to inoculate

There is no consensus as to the optimum time to inoculate. It is a fact, however, that it is more difficult to get MLF started after fermentation is over, due to high alcohol, reduced nutrients and absence of heat from fermentation. It is also a fact that the mal-olactic bacteria very much like the presence of skins. So in the case of red wines, I always add the malolactic starter and yeast extract as soon as fermentation reaches its peak, which is usually two days after the yeast starter was added. If the ML starter is added right after the onset of fermentation and the wine temperature is main-tained, MLF is sometimes complete by the time you want to press in approximately two weeks, depending on the pH, tempertature and amount of malic acid.

Malolactic fermentation is not as easily induced in white wines since they are fermented cooler than reds, have fewer nutrients and are not fermented on the skins. It is particularly important to use yeast extract for MLF in white wines. In the case of Chardonnay, which is commonly fermented at 65° F (18° C), you could add the malolactic starter and yeast extract shortly after fermentation be-comes vigorous and hope to get it started during primary fermen-tation. My preference is to wait until the wine is dry and inoculate then. If you wait, I would suggest using a freeze dried strain, such as *Viniflora oenos*, because it is more dependable in still wines. By waiting you will end up with more diacetyl, the source of the buttery quality, because there will be no yeast activity to neutralize it. The trade-off in waiting is that it is more difficult to initiate MLF in still wines; and the longer you wait, the more uncertain the proposition becomes.

White wines are most successfully inoculated as soon as they are still. Do not rack off the lees as the lees are an important source of nutrient for the bacteria. Raise the temperature of the wine to 70-75° F (21-24° C), add 1/2 teaspoon per gallon of yeast extract or proprietary MLF nutrient, such as Leucofood®, and then stir in the MLF starter. A small packet of *Vinaflora oenos* will treat up to 60 gallons, which is approximately 1/8 teaspoon per 5 gallons. However, with a still wine, I would double that dosage. Keep it at 70-75° F (21-24° C), stir up the lees two or three times a week with a slender dowel, and you will eventually force it to completion. Note that a low pH wine will take longer to complete MLF than a high pH wine.

Malolactic fermentation will be easiest to initiate in the carboy having the most pulp and solids. Rather than making a starter, I often concentrate the pulp in one carboy and inoculate that carboy with the starter. Once MLF is established, a pint or quart of the sludge can be drawn out with a long wine thief and transferred to the other carboys. One package of starter can sometimes be made to work for much more than 5 gallons this way.

When is MLF complete?

It is important to know when MLF is complete because the temperature should be lowered as soon afterward as possible. The higher temperatures and lack of meta create a high risk of undesirable side reactions. This risk is drastically reduced when the temperature is lowered and meta added. You also want to know whether or not the conversion is complete before bottling as renewed malolactic activity in the bottle could ruin the wine.

There are several ways to determine when all the malic acid has been converted to lactic, the simplest being to watch the bubble activity closely. MLF generates tiny bubbles of CO_2. Give the carboy a quick twist and a rush of small bubbles is a good indication of malolactic activity, particularly if Clinitest indicates that the wine is bone dry. If the conditions were right, and it appeared that MLF started, and the temperature has been constantly maintained at 65° F (18° C) or more, the conversion will probably be complete when the bubbles slow noticeably or stop. This is an acceptable method of monitoring MLF, although not the most reliable.

You could supplement bubble watching with periodic titration tests, which will indicate reductions in total acidity. When total acid stops falling and the bubbles slow or stop, MLF is presumably complete, again assuming proper conditions and a temperature continuously above 65° F (18° C).

Paper chromatography is the best way of testing for completion of MLF. A test kit is not prohibitively expensive or difficult to use (see *appendix A*). With red wines, a test should be run as soon as it is dry. Occasionally, MLF will be complete by then, in which case the wine should immediately be racked, sulfited and chilled to reduce the risk of spoilage. If MLF is not complete, hold the temperature at 70-75° F (21-24° C) until it finishes, which will usually be another month or two.

Once you have malolactic fermentation underway, do your utmost to get it go to completion without interruption. Keep the temperature up and stir up the lees twice weekly with a slender dowel. It is not only a matter of wanting to finish MLF so that the wine can be cold stabilized during the depth of winter — you want to avoid the risk of renewed MLF after bottling. If you let the temperature fall, for instance, malolactic fermentation would stop, but the bacteria will not die, even if you sulfite. Activity might or might not resume the following summer. If it does not, you might be forced to bottle with incomplete MLF, only to have it resume after bottling, even if you sulfited before bottling. With no way for the bacterial odor and gases to escape the bottle, the wine would probably be ruined. That's why it is good practice to run a chromatography test before bottling.

If a wine has gone through MLF and the acid drops so low that it has to be increased, be sure to use tartaric acid rather than malic. Malic acid would be an invitation to renewed activity. Don't use acid blend because they almost always contain some malic acid.

Stuck MLF

If malolactic fermentation appears to have stopped, but a chromatography test reveals the process to be only partially complete, it has stuck. This usually occurs when the wine was too cold for too long — it can be difficult to get it going again. Raise the temperature to 70-75° F (21-24° C) and add another 1/2 teaspoon of yeast extract or MLF nutrient of some type. Stir up the lees with your dowel two or three times a week, and it will probably start again. If it does not, add a fresh starter. Again, *Viniflora oenos*, is more dependable in still wines.

If you have tried everything and cannot get MLF to go to completion, go ahead and bottle anyway. The wine itself will not be inferior if most of the malic acid is converted. The risk of post-bottling MLF can be reduced if 75 ppm of meta is used at bottling. This is a fairly heavy dose which will give the bouquet a sulfite bite for a while, but it will disappear in a few months. The risk of post-bottling MLF can be further reduced if you have the means to super-chill the wine down to 25° F (-4° C) for a week or two, which tends to kill the bacteria. Fumaric acid added at the rate of 200 ppm will inhibit renewed MLF, but probably affect the flavor — do bench trials first.

The risk of post-bottling MLF can be totally eliminated by using 1 gram of lysozyme per gallon. See page 118.

Precautions

The absence of meta in combination with higher temperatures creates a situation that is ripe for spoilage problems. The wine should not be exposed to any air in this vulnerable state. The bit of CO_2 generated by MLF will protect it from air and acetobacter. Acetobacter, which cannot form without oxygen, is indicated by a white film or crust on the surface in the neck of the carboy. It is a precursor to vinegar and even trace amounts are objectionable. If a white crust does appear in the neck of the carboy, the best remedy is to insert a small tube into the wine, add a bit of water or sound wine and "float" the scum out of the carboy, as it is almost impossible to spoon or siphon it out. A tiny burette funnel and small tube make this procedure easier. Then rack, sulfite 50 ppm and cool. If a surface film does develop, just hope the wine is not already ruined. A heavy dose of meta might help deal with an off-flavor but there is no actual cure.

The risk of acetobacter can be reduced by occasionally adding a tablespoon of brandy in the neck of the carboy. Better yet, spray a mist of Everclear over the surface, as wineries do. The alcohol kills the bacteria.

If this is your first effort at home winemaking, I suggest that you wait a season or two before attempting malolactic fermentation, particularly in white wines. The limited use of sulfite and higher temperatures required to induce MLF greatly increase the risk of ruining your wine. Ultimately, you will probably opt to put all of your red table wines through malolactic fermentation. In addition to lowering total acidity, it eliminates the "bright, fruity" taste of malic acid, which most people find objectionable in red wines. As to white wines, the choice is less clear because MLF takes away some of the fruitiness, and the fruity flavor of malic acid can be a plus. On the other hand, MLF adds a buttery flavor that is generally regarded as a plus.

Malolactic Bacteria Glossary

Several different strains of cultured malolactic bacteria have been isolated and developed commercially. Most wine supply stores will carry one or two different strains. Some strains produce more diacetyl than others. Some work at lower pH than others, and some at lower temperatures. Here are some notes on those that are often available.

VINIFLORA OENOS by Chr. Hansen (Denmark). This is a very good product and is the best choice to inoculate a still wine. It can be added directly to the wine without the nuisance of having to make a starter solution several days before inoculating. It is freeze-dried and will keep a season or two in the freezer, as long as the foil packet has not been opened. Once opened, it should be used promptly as it is very sensitive to humidity. This is a good choice to induce MLF in a still Chardonnay. Add it after the wine is still to maximize the buttery quality. If added before fermentation is complete, the yeast will neutralize some of the diacetyl, which is the source of the buttery flavor.

UVAFERM MLD by Lallemand is another freeze-dried, direct-add culture. It comes in 3-gram packets sufficient for 55 gallons (227 liters).

OREGON STATE UNIVERSITY STRAIN. This strain was isolated for use on the low pH Pinot Noirs from Oregon's Willamette Valley. I like it not so much because it is said to work as low as 2.9 pH, but because it is more active in the 65-70° F (18-21° C) range. It is easier to maintain this temperature during winter months than 75-80° F (24-27° C), as required by the other strains. This strain is marketed by Lallemand as "OSU" and by Wyeast Laboratories, Mt. Hood, Oregon, as "Vintner's Choice." The latter is in liquid form in foil packets which can be added directly without making a starter solution. Vinquiry also markets it in 2-gram packets as "MCW."

LALLEMAND X-3. This is a good combination of four different strains. It comes in dried form (not freeze-dried), but making a starter solution is easy. Lallemand markets several other strains as well.

TWO-PART STARTERS. The traditional two-part, wet malolactic starter is the least expensive, but must be activated a week before inoculating and given time to completely convert all malic acid in the starter sample to lactic acid. Ideally, this would be confirmed by chromatography before inoculating because MLF is not likely to start unless the conversion is complete.

LYSOZYME. This casein derivative works by dissolving the cell walls of gram-positive bacteria and can be used to stop or delay the malolactic fermentation process. If, for instance, you were not able to get your wine fully through malolactic fermentation, lysozyme at the rate of 1 gram per U.S. gallon will prevent renewed MLF after bottling. Similarly, if you wanted to put a Chardonnay or Pinot Noir only partially through malolactic fermentation, you could stop the process at the desired point. Some wine makers routinely use it before barrel aging because it increases the stability of a finished wine. It can be used instead of sulfite at the rate of 1/2 gram per gallon to kill natural malolactic bacteria in red-grape musts. I routinely use it in high-pH wines to augment the sulfite. If you are struggling with a stuck primary fermentation, lysozyme (1 gram per gallon) will keep the volatile acid level from creeping up while you get the primary fermentation to go to completion at warmer temperatures. If you want to re-inoculate with a ML starter after using lysozyme, fine first with bentonite to remove the excess.

To prepare lysozyme, mix it into a bit of warm water and gently stir it into the wine. Stored dry and cool, lysozyme has excellent shelf life.

Chapter Thirteen

SPARKLiNG WiNES

parkling wines from the Champagne area of France are the only ones which can rightfully be called "champagne." However, fine sparkling wines come from many other parts of the world; and there is no reason your cellar could not be added to the list! The home winemaker can in fact make first class sparkling wines — far better than you ever expect. But you have to start with good fruit, and it takes patience. The technique described below — known to the French as *méthode champenoise* — is the best process there is for making sparkling wines, whether it be with Pinot Noir, Chardonnay, Riesling, peaches or apricots. The discussion that follows is in terms of white grape juice, but the same technique would work for peaches or apricots as long as the acid level is raised to .7% or more.

Méthode champenoise

The goal initially is to make a sound dry white table wine having alcohol in the range of 10 to 11%. The first fermentation is known as the *cuvée* fermentation and is done by home winemakers in carboys in essentially the same manner as set forth in chapter 2 for regular white table wines. Except that the grapes are picked when the sugar level is 18-20° Brix. After the *cuvée* has been fermented, racked and clarified, a measured amount of sugar and fresh yeast starter are added and the wine is bottled and capped.

The sugar ferments slowly in the bottle; it is this *tirage* fermentation which gives the wine its effervescence.

After the *tirage* fermentation, the wine is aged on the lees in the bottle for a period of time ranging from several months to several years. Then the bottles are "riddled." Riddling, or *remuage* to the French, is the process of manipulating the lees into the neck of the bottle with sharp twists of the bottle. The bottles are held at an angle in a rack and the angle is gradually increased until the rack is flat and the bottles vertical.

Next, a small plug of ice is frozen in the neck of the bottle to hold the lees in place. When the bottle is tipped to a 45° angle and the cap removed, the lees are blown out along with the ice plug. The wine is now "disgorged." A measured amount of sugar syrup — the *dosage* — is quickly added to sweeten the remaining wine. The bottle is then permanently closed. This is the essence of *méthode champenoise*, used by makers of fine sparkling wines throughout the world.

Grapes for sparkling wines

Although Pinot Noir and Chardonnay are the classic grape types for French champagnes, other varieties also work well, including Semillon, Sauvignon Blanc and Riesling or blends thereof. Grapes for sparkling wines are picked at an earlier stage of ripeness — typically between 18 and 20° Brix — in order to produce a still wine with only 10-11% alcohol before bottle fermentation. A lower level of alcohol is desired because sugar will be added for bottle fermentation, and that will raise the alcohol level to the desired level of 13% or so. If you started with grapes having a Brix of 24°, the wine would have 13% alcohol after the *cuvée* fermentation. It would be difficult to initiate bottle fermentation with 13% alcohol; and even if successful, the finished wine would have alcohol of 14½% after bottle fermentation. That is too high. So it works best to use grapes having a Brix of 18 to 20°.

Ideally, total acid of the grapes would be .75-.80%, but the acid usually will not have dropped to that level when the sugar is still below 20° B. So acid of 1% or more is to be expected when grapes are picked at 18-20° Brix. Higher acid can be countered with a higher level of residual sugar when the dosage is added.

Crushing and pressing

White grapes, such as Chardonnay, are crushed, pressed and processed as though you were setting out to make a typical dry white table wine, as described in chapter 2. However, if you are processing red grapes, such as Pinot Noir, you will need to decide before crushing whether you want a sparkling white wine, a blush or a rosé. Although Pinot Noir grapes are red, the juice is white. But if crushed and left on the skins, the wine will absorb pigment from the skins. The higher the alcohol level, the faster the juice will become colored. Coloration can be completely avoided if the grapes are pressed without first being crushed. The resulting white wine is known and marketed as *"blanc de noirs"* to distinguish it from a *"blanc de blancs"* made from white grapes.

On the other hand, if you want enough color that a blush wine will result, the grapes should be crushed and soaked on the skins for a while and then pressed and fermented. If you want an even darker, rosé-type sparkling wine, crush, de-stem and ferment on the skins for a short while before pressing. The higher the alcohol, the more quickly the color is leached out of the skins.

Many champagne producers press only lightly for their premium bottlings without crushing first. The lightly-pressed pomace is then crushed and pressed again to make a sparkling wine of somewhat lesser quality. Blending of varieties and vintages is also common, particularly in the Champagne region of France, where some varieties do not ripen sufficiently every year.

Whether processing red grapes or white grapes, meta should be carefully limited to 50 parts per million at pressing. This will be sufficient to discourage malolactic fermentation which is not desired in sparkling wines. Since grapes of this type are typically low in tannin, I like to add $1/4$ - $1/2$ tsp. of tannin per 5 gallons at pressing as an aid in clarifying.

Although almost any strain of yeast could be used for the *cuvée* fermentation, I am partial to cold fermenting with Steinberg yeast when working with Pinot Noir or Chardonnay to preserve as much of the fruit and bouquet as possible.

Cuvée fermentation

The *cuvée* fermentation takes place in carboys filled to about 3/4 capacity and topped with air locks. When unfermented sugar is nearing 0° B., the carboys are combined or topped up and the temperature raised to about 70° to encourage complete fermentation. When Clinitest confirms that it is dry, the carboys should be topped up again if necessary and the wine cold stabilized for one to two months.

Racking, fining and clarifying

The challenge of clarifying is the same as it is with any white wine. Follow the procedures in chapter 2, with one exception. Since you want no free SO_2 in solution when the *tirage* yeast is added for bottle fermentation, meta should be omitted entirely at the last racking. This is when the wine is reinoculated with a fresh yeast starter, bottled and *tirage* fermentation initiated. Everything else is the same.

You would like the wine to be crystal clear before the sugar is added for bottle fermentation because if it isn't clear by then, you'll never be able to clear it in the bottle. If the second fining attempt is not a total success and the wine has been cold stabilized for several months, proceed with bottle fermentation anyway. The haze will be an aesthetic negative but will not diminish the flavor.

Choice of bottles

Whether you plan to purchase new bottles or soak labels off used bottles and clean them up, they should be heavy sparkling wine bottles of U.S. origin, free of chips or flaws. Avoid sparkling cider bottles and any that are not heavy enough to withstand the high pressure that will build up after bottle fermentation. Bottles made in the U.S. are preferable because the neck is the right diameter to accommodate a standard crown cap such as is used for beer or soda pop. Rather than inserting a mushroom cork or plastic cap, U.S. sparkling wine producers simply cap the bottles with a crown cap for the *tirage* fermentation. You want to be able to do the same, since a crown cap is much easier to put on and take off. Bottles from Spain, France and Italy have a larger neck diameter which a crown cap will not fit.

Bottles having any stain or mold in them should also be discarded — they're not worth the effort. It is important that bottles for sparkling wines be carefully cleaned with a brush to remove any stain or invisible film they may contain. The cleaner the glass, the more freely the sediment will slip down into the neck of the bottle when it is riddled.

Bottling and *tirage* fermentation

After several months of cold stabilization and two or perhaps three rackings, the *cuvée* wine will be totally dry and hopefully crystal clear. It will be either white or blush as planned and will have alcohol in the 10 to 11% range. Total acid will have dropped slightly from its pre-fermentation level. Other types of wine might have been blended along the way if you had them on hand and felt experimental.

The procedure for making sparkling wines now departs from that for dry white table wines: it is time to add a measured amount of sugar, inoculate with a fresh yeast starter and bottle the wine for the *tirage* fermentation. The more sugar you add, the more carbonated the wine will be. Add too much, and you'll have bottles exploding all over the place! So the amount of sugar has to be carefully measured to stay within the limits of the bottle strength.

Although champagne bottles will withstand pressures of 8 or 10 atmospheres, commercial winemakers seldom exceed 6 atmospheres of bottle pressure. It is better for the home winemaker to limit it to 4 atmospheres. This will provide an abundance of carbonation without running the risk of exploding bottles. In fact, there would be nothing wrong with adding only enough sugar to produce two atmospheres of pressure and ending up with a creamy, spritzy wine known in France as a *crémant*. The amount of carbonation and the alcohol level are far less important in the case of sparkling wines than is the quality of the grapes and the time spent on the lees.

Four grams of sugar per liter will generate one atmosphere of pressure after bottle fermentation. To produce four atmospheres, therefore, you will need 16 grams of sugar per liter. This is the equivalent of $2^{1}/_{8}$ ounces per gallon. Before doing the calculations, do another Clinitest just to make sure there is no unfermented sugar left in the wine. If there is, convert the percentage to grams or ounces and deduct it from your calculations.

It will be more difficult to initiate the *tirage* fermentation than the initial fermentation. In addition to 10 or 11% alcohol, the wine has been clarified and has a low nutrient level compared to the original must. This combination of factors creates a rather hostile atmosphere in which to re-initiate fermentation. So it has to be done with some care. Here is how to handle this critical stage.

Choice of yeast is important for bottle fermentation. You want a yeast which is vigorous and alcohol-tolerant, making Prise de Mousse a good choice. Surprisingly, Pasteur Champagne is not recommended. California Champagne yeast (UCD #505) would be an excellent choice since it coagulates and clears so readily; but it is difficult to locate. So you will probably find yourself using Prise de Mousse.

Before activating the yeast, a sugar syrup should be made by dissolving a carefully calculated and weighed amount of cane or beet sugar ($10^1/_2$ ounces per 5 U.S. gallons/19 liters of wine) in an equal volume of warm water or wine. Heat it gently in the micro-wave if necessary to dissolve it. Set the syrup aside to cool.

Now activate two packets of the dry yeast in four ounces of warm water as explained in chapter 2. After the yeast is rehydrated, rack the *cuvée* into a large pail or primary fermenter and add the sugar syrup and activated yeast plus $^1/_2$ tsp. of diammonium phosphate per 5 gallons. Also add about 2 ounces of liquid beermaker's isinglass. The isinglass will help clarification after bottle fermentation by coagulating with the yeast hulls. You can also add another $^1/_4$ to $^1/_2$ tsp. of tannin at this time, dissolved in water, because most of the tannin that was previously added will have precipitated with the first dose of isinglass. And some of the tannin being added now will precipitate with the additional isinglass being added. Any excess will oxidize during the years it spends on the lees.

After everything is mixed up in the pail and stirred a bit for aeration, the wine should be immediately racked into the champagne bottles, which should previously have been thoroughly washed, brushed and rinsed. Use your dowel to stir up the yeast in the pail occasionally while racking — solids tend to settle rather quickly and you want some yeast in each bottle.

Leave about an inch of air space in each bottle. Use a bottle capper to seal the bottles with crown caps, and mark the side of each bottle with a piece of masking tape or paint stripe. This reference point is needed so the bottles can be returned to the same position each time after being shaken during the months to come.

The bottles should be stored at 55-60° F (13-16° C), not over 65° F (18° C), for two or three months while bottle fermentation takes place. Shake each bottle once a week for the first month to disperse the yeast and return it to the same position, tape marker up. It is always advisable to wear protective goggles and gloves while shaking bottles in case one is cracked or has a flaw. After three months, bottle fermentation should be complete, but the time can vary. Test a bottle to be sure it is bone dry.

The natural desire is to get on with the process so you can start drinking your wine! But you will be well rewarded by waiting. A goodly portion of the high price tag on vintage champagnes from France is attributable to the time spent on the lees, which could be up to six or seven years. During this period of time the yeast cells die and decompose, which imparts a pleasing flavor. A distinct change in character is said to occur after two years on the lees and another after four or five years. In any event the wine should spend at least one year on the lees before being riddled and disgorged, simply to allow ample time for all the yeast cells to die and settle out. The bottles should be shaken two or three times a year during this time and replaced in the same position, marker up.

Riddling

Aside from a bottle capper, the only additional equipment needed for making sparkling wines is a riddling rack (See *Illustration E*, next page, for hole diameters and spacing using a standard two–by–two and 1/2" plywood for the frame). The type of rack or method of construction is not important, but it should be designed with a pivot point so that the angle can be changed as riddling progresses. A small rack sufficient for 12 bottles should suffice. I built a huge one capable of holding 48 bottles and later discovered that I riddle and disgorge only a case at a time. The longer it takes to get around to building your rack, the more time the wine will have on the lees; so there's no great rush on this project!

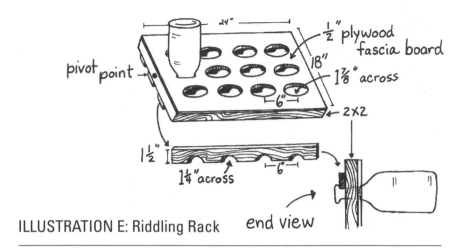

ILLUSTRATION E: Riddling Rack   end view

When riddling is started, the bottles will be almost horizontal. By the end of riddling, the board will be horizontal and the bottles standing vertically, neck down, with the lees accumulated on the crown cap. Start the riddling process by vigorously shaking each bottle to loosen the lees and stain that accumulated during aging. Because the bottles were faithfully replaced with the tape marker up, the sediment will be limited to one location. Place the bottles, stain now dissolved, in the rack, with the rack positioned so that the bottles rest at about 30° above horizontal. Use the tape marker to place them all in the same relative position.

After a few days the lees will have settled again — it's time for the first riddling installment. Give each bottle a sharp twist 90° in one direction, immediately followed by a sharp twist 45° back toward the original position. Drop it back in the slot with a small jolt which will help break the lees loose from the glass.

This process should be repeated every two or three days until the tape marker indicates that the bottles have been rotated a full 360°. Then change the angle of the rack so that the bottles are closer to upright. Increase the bottle angle to perhaps 45° and repeat the process until they have been rotated another full 360°. Then increase the bottle angle another notch. As the angle gets steeper, the lees will slide toward the neck more willingly and you can rotate them more than +90°/-45° each time. There will ultimately be about one teaspoon of yeast lees and isinglass resting in the neck of each bottle. Once riddled, the bottles can be stored indefinitely, neck down, or you can proceed at once with disgorging.

Disgorging, adding the *dosage* and recapping

The object in disgorging is to freeze an ice plug in the neck of the bottle, pop the cap to blow it out, add a measured quantity of sugar syrup to sweeten the wine and recap the bottle. The method I ultimately settled upon for freezing the ice plug is a plywood rack in the freezer. A piece of $1/2$ inch plywood with holes (about $1^3/_8 - 1^1/_2$" diameter) drilled on six inch centers works well; you might even be able to use the board from your riddling rack. Devise legs as needed to prop up the board in the freezer after it has been loaded with several bottles of wine.

If the freezer is full, chill the wine in a refrigerator for a day. Then get a hefty supply of crushed ice and sprinkle a generous quantity of calcium chloride on the ice to lower the freezing point and stick the necks of the bottles in. I have not tried this, but it would probably work if done on a cold winter day.

I suggest freezing only one bottle initially. Some of this bottle will be used to make the sugar syrup, or *dosage*, and the rest to top up the remaining bottles after the *dosage* is added. Check regularly to determine approximately how long it will take for an ice plug $1^1/_2$ to 2 inches long to form. If the ice plug is much longer, you will lose too much wine when the cap is popped off.

After the ice plug has formed, cradle the bottle in the crook of your arm at a 45° angle and pop the cap off. The ice plug encapsuling the lees will disappear instantly, taking the lees with it, and you will end up with almost 750 ml of clear sparkling wine which is bone dry. Cap this first bottle with a stopper to retain the sparkle and store it in the refrigerator.

While the other 11 bottles are in the freezer, make the *dosage*. How much sugar to add? This takes us back to the topic of residual sugar/total acid discussed in chapter 3! It's matter of acid level and preference. A "brut" champagne of French origin might have residual sugar of up to 1.5%, a "sec" up to 2.5% and a "demi-sec" up to 4 or 5%. So ultimately it depends on your palate.

Assuming that a Clinitest confirms the wine to be totally dry, that you want residual sugar of 1%, and that you will be disgorging 11 bottles, you will need to add about 3 ounces of sugar per 11 bottles (750 ml X 11 X .01 = 82.5 g. = 2.9 ounces). Weigh out the needed amount of sugar and add it to a slightly smaller volume of wine from the first bottle. Better yet, use a good quality brandy. My container of choice is a measuring cup or beaker marked in milliliters. Now gently warm the sugar solution in the microwave as necessary to dissolve the sugar, stir, warm again, stir.

Until now, the yeast lees, which have a very high affinity for oxygen, have been protecting the wine against oxidation. Once the lees are removed, the wine will need some protection in the form of SO_2. When the sugar has dissolved and the syrup cooled, dissolve $1/8$ tsp. of potassium metabisulfite in 11 ml of water. One ml per bottle will raise the level of free SO_2 to about 50 parts per million. This is a bit on the high side and might be detectable right after adding the *dosage* and recorking, particularly since the effervescence will lift it right into your nostrils. However, the free SO_2 will quickly bond to the sugar and will not be noticeable after a few months. It is needed to give your sparkling wine some much needed protection against oxidation. If no sulfite is added at this stage, madeirization will probably be noticeable in less than a year.

Divide the total volume of sugar syrup in the beaker or measuring cup by 11 to determine the amount of syrup to be added to each bottle. I use a 10 ml oral dispenser from the drug store to draw out the correct volume of syrup and dispense it into each bottle after it has been opened and disgorged. Also add 1 ml of the sulfite solution with a pipet. Now the bottle should be topped up with dry sparkling wine from the first bottle and quickly corked or capped. Keep the first bottle capped and chilled when not in use to minimize loss of carbonation.

Corking

The classic mushroom-shaped cork is the best closure device but requires a special corker which is a relatively big expense for the limited use it will probably receive. Most home winemakers will be content to use a plastic closure, which can be driven in with a rubber mallet and held in place with a wire basket. Or you could use another crown cap — not very classy, but it will do a good job of retaining pressure and keeping air out. Crimp a foil capsule over the neck and the work is done—at last!

As you know by now, *méthode champenoise* is time consuming and labor intensive. If you are willing to make the commitment, consider doubling or tripling the quantity of grapes you normally process. Particularly if high quality fruit at 18° to 19° Brix is available to you. That way, you can enjoy some of the wine while the rest continues to age on the lees. Larger quantities will also allow you to lightly press some of the grapes without crushing and to make a second wine from heavily pressed grapes. If you decide that the sugar level in the first batch to be disgorged and sweetened is either too high or too low, it can be corrected for the next batch. The key to premium champagne, once again, is starting with premium fruit and aging on the lees.

Chapter Fourteen

ALL ABOUT OAK

ak has captured the fancy of winemakers and wine drinkers for many generations, and it continues to do so. It was once the only practical container material for fermenting and transporting wine but is now thought of as a way to enhance wine quality. An immense amount of research is being conducted on every imaginable aspect of the wood. This has led to greatly improved knowledge, better wines and more efficient use of a limited resource.

Oak, in my opinion, is a valuable asset in making all but the aromatic wines. Even someone who abhors highly-oaked wines should consider using it, but at a very low level, because oak does wonders to pull the acids, alcohol, tannins, and glycerine into harmony. If you are concerned about the loss of delicate fruit flavors, then give it only a short exposure to oak. The oak bouquet and flavor will dissipate in a few months, resulting in a wine that is more balanced and cohesive, with little loss in fruit.

Oak affects a wine in a variety of ways. It adds another dimension to the bouquet and flavor; it increases volatile acidity and total acidity; it lowers the pH; it releases tannins and other phenols into the wine; and it adds to the wine's overall complexity. The flavors and bouquet of caramel, coconut, vanilla, roasted nuts, and cinnamon, for example, emanate from the wood, not the fruit. Although the ultimate effect depends on many factors, wood quality and toasting are the two most important variables, recognizing, of course, that nothing will ever compensate for inferior fruit quality.

The wood used in winemaking is at least 100 years old and some of it is closer to 200 years old — it takes that long to reach the requisite 24-inch diameter. The tree is felled and allowed to dry in place for several months. Then it is transported to the mill, cut into usable size and stacked outside for drying. It is critical that the wood be air-dried. Air-dried wood has a denser cellular alignment and imparts better flavors than kiln-dried wood. The longer it is air-dried, the softer the tannins and the sweeter the flavors. It should be exposed to the elements for at least two winters and some wineries insist on three seasons, particularly for American oak, which has a more forward flavor than French oak. It even makes a difference where the oak is dried. Most American oak is dried in the Midwest, where the relative humidity is high enough to support the growth of mold and fungus on the wood. This consumes some of the harsh tannins and other phenols and sweetens the wood for purposes of aging wine.

Toasting technique is equally critical. Subjecting the oak to carefully controlled heat for limited period of time breaks down the cellulose and lignin. If the heat is too intense or held too long or if the heat source (usually scrap oak) is contaminated, the flavors and bouquet will suffer. Fortunately, American oak is now being toasted by skilled craftsmen. As more French firms have established subsidiaries in the U.S. and bought American firms, the French have lost the advantage in coopering they held a generation ago.

There are three general levels of toasting, and the wine will be different depending on which one is used. Which toast is to be used for which wine is completely the vintner's choice. **Medium Toast** has a high concentration of vanilla which affects flavor more than bouquet. Less tannin is extracted with medium toast, so that a wine can be exposed to it for a longer period of time. Longer wood contact is beneficial in that it allows for better linking of tannin molecules, known as polymerization. The longer the exposure, the longer the chains of tannin molecules and the softer the effect. Medium toast has traditionally been used for heavy red wines because they seem to benefit from longer wood contact.

Medium Plus toast is darker brown in color and delivers the aromas of coffee, caramel and roasted nuts. It is used for Chardonnay and Pinot Noir as well as heavy red wines. I particularly like its toasty flavor in Pinot Noir.

Heavy Toast is not as common, but it does exist and can be used. It imparts a pronounced toasty flavor very quickly, so you have to monitor the situation very carefully. I sometimes use it for a short while after extended aging in medium toast. After the wine has sufficient oak flavor, I add some heavily toasted chips to give it a carbonized overlay. The wine picks up the toasty quality very quickly, and I remove it before much more oak flavor is added. This way, I get tannin polymerization from long-term contact with medium toast plus the toasty quality from a heavier toast. Overall, you sacrifice a lot of flexibility with heavy toast, so its use should be limited to special situations.

Oak species

French oak (*Quercus robur* and *Quercus sessiliflora*) is the most highly regarded source. It has been used in cooperage for many generations and is farmed in several forests in central France, most notably *Allier*, *Nevers*, *Vosges*, *Troncais* and *Limousin*. High worldwide demand has driven the price of French oak to prohibitive levels for ordinary wines, but it is highly sought after for use in making premium wines. French oak imparts a more subtle flavor than American oak and less oak bouquet. It adds more tannins, raises total acid more and lowers pH slightly more than American oak. The two species of French oak are interchangeable — the tightness of the grain is a bigger factor than which of the two species is used. Both species are grown in all of the French forests.

American oak (*Quercus alba*) is a tight-grained species of white oak that produces a more distinct aroma than French oak and imparts an oak flavor faster than French oak. But it usually softens faster. Due to previous shortcomings in methods of drying, toasting and coopering, American oak developed a reputation for being inferior to French oak. However, methods of processing and coopering American oak have improved so immensely during the past decade or two that it can no longer be categorically said that French is better than American. Given extra air drying, American oak is every bit as good as French. The two are simply different, and the choice of one over the other depends on the vintner's preference. Many thousands of American oak barrels are now exported to France each year for use in making French wines.

American oak comes from the Midwest, as far south as Missouri and Kentucky, east to Virginia and as far north as Michigan. No matter what state or country, the colder the climate, the slower the tree will grow and the tighter the grain will be. Tighter-grained oak from Michigan, for example, can be expected to release flavors more slowly and allow for longer wine contact than a more porous wood from Kentucky.

Hungarian oak (*Quercus petraea, robur*) is essentially the same as French oak, but is less expensive. In my opinion, it is a better value than French oak.

Oregon oak (*Quercus Garryana*) is gaining favor as wineries look for new and better species of oak, and hopefully less expensive ones. Some wineries use it almost exclusively. It delivers a floral quality that distinguishes it slightly from French oak, but the two are very similar in most respects.

Barrel alternatives

As you can see, the choices are many when it comes to oak. It's easy to get enthused about the various oak types and toasts and imagining how they will improve your wine. But if you want to learn the art of applying oak to wine, bear in mind that the quality of the wood and manner in which it is used count more than anything else. The species of oak makes some difference but it is secondary. My suggestion, if you are a relative newcomer, is that you limit the variables until you have developed a good feel for the product you are using and what you like in the wine varieties that you tend to specialize in. The last thing a beginner needs is three or four different oak types in two or three toast levels. Buy one French oak and one American oak, both in medium toast. Or, a medium toast and medium plus toast, both of the same species and source. Then do side-by-side carboys so that each time you can compare and add to your knowledge base. You will learn faster this way than with the very tempting "scatter-gun" approach.

It is difficult for a home winemaker to systematically add to her knowledge base by using barrels because the barrel cost and wine quantities are prohibitive. You need more side-by-side comparisons than one or two barrels would allow. In addition, the second wine through a barrel will not be the same as the first. It makes more sense to start out with barrel alternatives. Whether that be beans or staves or chips does not matter as long as the quality of the wood is high. Use the same product(s) for several seasons and after you know what you like and don't like, then add a new variable, such as a new species or toast.

This approach is not as confining as it might seem. There are enough different ways you can use two products to keep the learning process interesting. For instance, you could break in beans or staves by using them during the primary fermentation of white wines, such as Chardonnay or Sauvignon Blanc. Leave them in the primary fermentation for a few days. As soon as the oak flavor seems too strong, remove the staves or rack off the beans or chips, as the case may be. Then immediately transfer the wood to a red wine.

This is essentially what wineries are doing when they break in new barrels by barrel fermenting white wines and then using them for longer term aging of red wines. By taking the edge off in white wine, oak-wine contact can be maintained longer, hopefully for the 6 to 9 months required to get optimum polymerization of the tannins. The reason new wood can be used this way without overwhelming a white wine is that the yeast metabolizes some of the oak elements. In addition, some of the oak tannins and flavors attach to the fermenting yeast cells and precipitate. But you still have to be careful. To avoid over-oaking their Chardonnay, some wineries will ferment a Semillon or Sauvignon Blanc in their new barrels for three or four days, then barrel ferment Chardonnay and finally use them for long-term aging of red wines.

There is no way to articulate when to stop oak contact in a wine. In part, it depends on personal preference. It's something you learn by experience. There will be a pronounced flavor after a week, which will integrate and diminish. Then the flavor will come on quickly after several more weeks or months of contact. The process requires your vigilance.

After bottling, the oak flavor will decrease markedly during the first year and somewhat during the second year. Note that the heavier the toast, the less the effect will diminish, due to the additional carbon. Until you develop a sense of how much the flavor will diminish over the course of one or two years, err on the short side to avoid over-oaking.

When purchasing oak, always pay the premium price necessary to get quality oak. You are not going to get quality oak for a dollar a pound. The first time I used high quality oak, I tasted my wines a week later in amazement and said to myself, "It's the wood, stupid, not barrels." I had always assumed that the distinct oak quality in commercial wines was the result of barrel aging. In reality, the quality of the oak and the toasting are far more important than the form of the oak. In my case the staves and beans I used were distinctly superior to the various chips and splinters I had previously been using, some of which had not even been toasted and left a green taste. Since you have no choice but to trust the source, buy from a reputable one. Several reputable barrel manufacturers, listed in *appendix G*, make their products available to wine supply shops and, in some cases, direct to home winemakers.

I am familiar with only two possible sources and have been impressed with the quality of both. StaVin has become a popular source of barrel alternatives for home winemakers as well as commercial. In addition to barrels, they have several products and systems, such as food-grade stainless steel mesh sleeves filled with oak "beans," as StaVin calls them. The sleeves can be inserted through the bung and suspended in an older barrel which has lost all its oak flavor or in larger stainless steel containers. The "beans" are cubes (approximately 7-8 mm, or 3/8 inch, thick) that have been toasted to one of the three standard degrees — medium, medium plus or heavy. They come in three different oak types—French, American and

StaVin beans, about the size of a dime, add oak flavor to old barrels.

"European," which I assume is Hungarian.

If you bulk age in carboys, buy StaVin's beans, not the inserts or sleeves. The company recommends use of about 2 1/2-3 oz. of new beans per 5 gallons. They also recommend leaving them in for two months. My preference is to start with less so that they can be left in longer. You can add a few more beans a few months later. Then a few more, always monitoring the taste. Using less oak will allow for longer contact and better polymerization.

Innerstave has a very high quality product called Chain-O-Oak. Each package contains 17 staves, again about 7-8 mm thick. The staves can be linked together, dropped into a barrel or tank and retrieved when the oak flavor starts getting too strong. As packaged, the staves are too wide to fit through the neck of a carboy. But they can be sawed or split down the middle.

Innerstave recommends 1 1/2 staves per 5 gallons (.08 staves per liter). However, these staves have so much oak character that

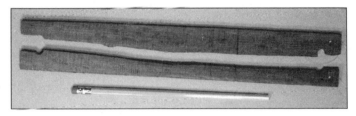

Staves are also used to boost oak flavor. One stave per 5 gallons is adequate.

I would recommend using only one stave (2 halves) per 5 gallons. The cost of French oak is only slightly higher than American oak and works out to approximately 15¢ a bottle, which is comparable to StaVin beans. One advantage of staves is that a hole can be drilled in each stave after splitting so it can be suspended with fish line and easily pulled out and transferred to another carboy without having to rack. You can retain the same control with beans by suspending them in a small nylon sock.

These staves and beans are sized so that all of the oak character gets extracted. Wine penetrates oak about 3 to 4 mm. With exposure on both sides (6 sides in the case of cubes), the oak flavor and tannins will be extracted in 9 or 10 months.

The reason I suggest beans, staves or chips rather than jumping right into barrels is that these alternatives will deliver at least 90% of the benefits of oak without the expense or contamination risk of barrels. If the lure of a barrel later becomes irresistible, then you will at least know the type of oak and toast that you prefer for your wine varieties and styles. In addition, the flavoring life of an oak barrel is limited. Almost all of the oak flavor will have been extracted from the standard 225-liter barrel by the end of three years of continuous use. Yet, a barrel will last for 8 or 10 years as a container if properly cared for. The home winemaker faces the same dilemma as the commercial vintner — the oak flavor is gone before the barrel's utility as a storage container is gone. The obvious solution is to use alternative oak sources, such as staves. Wineries commonly do this in their older barrels, and I doubt that the quality is significantly diminished.

Selecting a barrel

If you want the maximum benefit from oak, then you are talking about barrels. I have yet to encounter anyone who contends that staves, beans or other alternatives will equal a barrel of comparable quality wood. The wine picks up a little oxygen each time the bung is removed for tasting, testing or topping up. In addition, the fruit flavors intensify from transpiration and repeated topping up. That is, the water and alcohol evaporate but the solids and flavors remain, and more get added by topping up. In short, if you want the full potential of oak, then you have no choice but to use barrels.

Aside from type of oak and degree of toasting, barrel size is the biggest decision for the home winemaker. The optimum size for winemaking in terms of surface-to-volume ratio is the 225-liter size. But it takes about 1,100 pounds of grapes to fill it, including the 10% reserve that will be needed for topping up. That is a lot of wine for all but the wine clubs and groups. For that reason the 30 and 15 gallon sizes are more popular with home winemakers. The surface-to-volume ratio goes up as the barrel size decreases but is not prohibitive, even at the 15 gallon level. The increase in surface-to-volume ratio means only that you have to be more alert to possible over-oaking and that the risk of oxidation is higher.

Breaking in a barrel

First, make sure that your new barrel has a sweet oak aroma and that there are no construction flaws or problems, inside or out. A flashlight with a gooseneck head helps in examining the interior. The ends of all smaller barrels and many 55-gallon barrels will not be planed or toasted, which could influence your initiation of the barrel.

Although no two barrel manufacturers or wineries will have the same regimen for barrel treatment, they would all agree that a

225 liter oak barrel.

new barrel does not need to be cleaned with harsh chemicals. It was made with clean wood and then toasted to a high temperature, so there is no need for chemicals. Soap would only soften the wood; and soda ash, chemicals or even hot water would leach out some of the precious oak flavor and weaken the bung stave, which is the most vulnerable part of the barrel.

A new barrel should, however, be hydrated with care. If the wood is subjected to too much water too abruptly, it could swell abnormally and warp. The most conservative approach is to fill it

$1/_3$ full with cold water and allow it to swell for four hours. Then fill it to the $2/_3$ level. After four more hours, fill it to the top and allow it to swell until it stops leaking. If it is still leaking after three days, empty it and refill it with fresh water. This is to guard against the growth of bacteria and microbes which could result using unsulfited, high-pH water. It is rare that a modern day barrel will still be leaking after three days of soaking, but it could happen. If so, I would take it back!

In general, stick with cold water unless there is some specific reason for doing otherwise. For example, if the ends have not been toasted, as will be the case with smaller barrels, you might want to give the ends a warm water soak, particularly if you plan to age white wines. Stand the barrel on end after the gradual hydration discussed above and use a warm water soak (90-100° F.) of about 10% of the barrel volume. This will help reduce the harshness of the green oak. After a day or two of soaking, empty it, invert it and give the other end a soak. Similarly, if you are putting a used barrel back into circulation for the first time and are uncertain of its history, fill it with 90-100° F. water. After the temperature has dropped to 65°, drain it and immediately refill it with warm water, drain at 65°, etc. If you detect any off odors after three or four repetitions, maybe it would be best to take it back to the prior owner rather than risking your wine. If leakage is the problem and it continues to leak, check these articles on maintenance and repair: *Vineyard and Winery Management*, Jan./Feb, 1996, pp 27-30; *Practical Winery & Vineyard*, March/April, 1990, pp 41-42.

Using the barrel

Barrels are best located in a cool, humid corner of the basement or garage. Before filling the barrel, test the free sulfite in the wine and adjust as necessary while racking. Some winemakers treat their wines with lysozyme before barrel aging to increase the stability of the wine and decrease its vulnerability to microbial spoilage during barrel aging. Free sulfite should be maintained at 20-30 parts per million throughout bulk aging. Plan to top up once a week during the first month and once a month thereafter. A new barrel will soak up a surprising amount of reserved wine when it is first placed in use. Note that the more frequently you top up, the faster the wine will age. If you want to slow down the aging process, top up less than once a month, always using a silicone or Dynaflex bung to get the best possible seal. When the plug is removed, you should hear air rushing in to fill the vacuum. That little whoosh of air displacing the partial vacuum that built up will speed up aging. It is also reassurance that the barrel has been air tight.

Check the level of free sulfite three or four times a year and raise it as necessary to the 20-30 ppm minimum. Be aware that the level of free sulfite falls much faster in barrels than carboys and even faster in wines having a higher pH. The level of free sulfite is so critical in barrel- aging that you should invest in a vacuum aspiration setup. You have invested a great deal of money in the barrel and even more in its contents, so don't risk the investment by cutting corners with the Ripper method or Titrets, either of which always read high.

How long to oak?

There is no definitive answer to this question because it depends on so many variables, such as the age of the barrel, whether it was previously used for barrel fermentation of white wines, whether red wine or white wine is to be aged, the type and toast of the oak, how frequently you top up, and your fondness for oak flavor. Barrel size also has to be factored in because the surface-to-volume ratio of a $7\frac{1}{2}$-gallon barrel is almost twice that of a 55-gallon barrel. My best advice is to taste every time you pull the bung to top up or test free sulfite, take notes, and realize that the oak flavor will go through cycles. The flavor will build up rapidly during the first week or two and then rather quickly integrate. It builds up again after several weeks or months — this is when you have to be alert and taste regularly. You can let the oak flavor develop a little further than you think you would like before racking or bottling because a significant amount will integrate during the next year or two, particularly with American oak. Your experience with chips and beans will help in this regard.

If you are breaking in a new barrel, you might want to barrel ferment a couple batches of white wine before deploying it for red wines. Wineries commonly barrel ferment Chardonnay wines first because it takes the harshness off the new oak, improves the white wine and facilitates longer oak contact for the red wines to follow. The resulting white wine is quite different than it would be if fermented in glass or stainless steel and then barrel aged. Taste at least weekly at the outset

Barrel fermenting first is not mandatory; but if you do not take the edge off the oak via barrel fermentation, you will have to monitor the oak flavor with extra vigilance. With a white table wine going into a new barrel for bulk aging, as opposed to barrel fermentation, you might want to taste it in as little as three days. At the opposite extreme, a very fruity red wine will handle many months in an oak barrel that has seen considerable use. That's because almost all of the tannins and flavors are extracted during the first 3 years of contact with wine.

Given the subjective nature of oak contact, you are likely to leave some wine in contact too long. The best solution for an over-oaked wine is blending with a reserve that has not been exposed to oak. If blending isn't an option, try fining with potassium caseinate, which will help remove some of the excess oak.

Cleaning the barrel

A barrel should be thoroughly washed and cleaned with cold water immediately after being emptied. If you cold fermented or cold stabilized in the barrel, removal of the tartrate crust can be a challenge. Again, avoid the temptation to use harsh chemicals. Before resorting to chemicals, try to dissolve the tartrates by filling the barrel with 90-100° F. water. Empty it after the temperature has dropped to 70° and then refill it. Only after several repetitions should harsh chemicals or a pressure sprayer be considered. The point is that an oak barrel is a piece of craftsmanship to be treated as gently as possible.

Once the barrel is clean, the best strategy, by far, is to keep it full of wine at all times, never leaving it empty for more than a few hours. The wood continues to hold a lot a wine after it has been emptied, and acetobacter will immediately start converting that wine into vinegar if given a few hours of exposure to air. If you have no wine to refill it, maybe you could "borrow" some for a few months. Your friend's wine would benefit from the bit of oak flavor which you sacrifice, and your barrel will be safer filled with trouble-free wine.

Barrel storage - dry

Most home winemakers will not find it feasible to keep all barrels full all of the time, especially if working with larger barrels or if one is dedicated solely to white wines. If you find yourself with an empty barrel and several days or months until it will be filled again, clean it as discussed in the previous section. Set it outside to drain for an hour, bung down. Then rotate the bung straight up and burn a dripless sulfur pastille or wick. (This should always be done outdoors). Suspend the pastille on a thin copper wire so that it will not come into contact with the wood. Half a pastille will suffice for a 30 or 15 gallon barrel. Stopper it with a silicone bung. Repeat this ritual every 30 days or at such earlier time as you smell an off-odor or cannot detect sulfite.

If your barrels are located in your cellar, chances are the humidity will exceed 60%, and the procedure discussed above will suffice. High humidity is particularly common in the eastern half of the United States. However, if you are located in an arid climate, or if your barrels are stored in an air conditioned environment, the procedure for maintaining an empty barrel should be modified slightly so the barrel does not dry out and leak. You still need to burn sulfur once a month. But the barrel should be filled with warm water (90-100° F.) every other month before burning the sulfur pastille. Fill it with warm water and empty it when the temperature has dropped to 70°. After draining it, bung down, for an hour, burn the sulfur and stopper with a silicone bung. This approach repeated every two months (with an intervening sulfur pastille) is better than storing the barrel long-term with a sulfite-citric acid solution, which would take a toll on the oak flavors over time.

Before putting a stored barrel back into use, it should be thoroughly rinsed with cold water to remove any debris from the burned sulfur and then gradually re-hydrated. If left in, the sulfur would be converted to hydrogen sulfide during barrel fermentation and that would be the beginning of a major headache.

Chapter Fifteen

CONCENTRATE KĪTS

he market for concentrate kits is booming! Modern food processing equipment and techniques have become highly sophisticated in recent years and have enabled musts to be condensed with minimal loss of flavor. Concentrate kits have little or none of the caramelized flavor associated with canned concentrates. The essence of the fruit is trapped as the base is gently reduced to the desired volume and then the essence is added back. Since modern processing techniques allow more of the grape to be retained, it makes sense nowadays to use higher fruit quality. Home winemakers can make enjoyable wines with concentrate kits any time of the year, no matter where they live. Very little equipment is needed, and the cost is reasonable. So the boom in Canada is quite understandable, and it is just underway in the United States.

There are numerous brands of these bagged and boxed products, all marketed by Canadian companies as far as I am aware. The grapes come from all over the world — Italy, France, Chile, Argentina, Australia, California and Washington being the most common sources. Most are packaged to make 23 liters of finished wine, which is 5 Imperial gallons or 6 U.S. gallons. Those that have been concentrated the least are packaged in 15-liter boxes; you add 8 liters of water to bring the total to 23 liters. The next level down is packaged in 5 to 7 kilogram boxes to which considerably more water must be added to bring the total to 23 liters. Some companies also sell undiluted aseptic juice in 23-liter boxes. No water is added—just add yeast and ferment. Most concentrate companies also market a variety of exotic specialty wines packaged to make smaller quantities of finished wine.

Bear in mind that concentrate kits are subject to the same old rule: the better the grapes, the better the wine. These producers have to line up their sources of supply and make commitments early in the summer, the same as wineries. Sometimes the grapes will be great and sometimes they will be below average. With the grapes coming from all over the world at different times of the year and typically being blended as well, it becomes impossible to conclude that one brand is better than another. Each will have some good ones in the pipeline at any given time and some not so good.

Once you understand the basic procedure of chapter 2 for fermenting white wines and chapter 6 for red wines, there is little more to be said about fermenting concentrate kits. All fermentations are basically the same. The kits come packaged with yeast and additives needed to ferment and clarify. You don't even need a crusher or press, just a primary fermenter, carboys, racking hose and stem, etc. Follow the enclosed instructions, minimize the exposure to air, and you can expect 30 bottles of enjoyable wine. Use meta very sparingly as these kits are heavily sulfited and will not accommodate as much meta as fresh fruit.

You might find white wines from kits to be more difficult to clarify than wines from fresh grapes. The kits all come with one or two fining agents and directions which have undoubtedly been carefully tested. If you are not completely successful in clarifying your wine, don't worry about it as the residual haze is innocuous and will not affect the flavor.

The more concentrated the juice, the faster the wine will age. The 7-kg. boxes are marketed as "28-day" wines, and the 15-liter boxes as "6-week" wines. The aseptic juices are marketed as "six month" wines. Be aware that these are optimistic figures as every one of them will improve with additional aging.

In my opinion the future for concentrate kits looks very bright for home winemakers. I say this because the processing technology and equipment will continue to be refined. A few processors are starting to use spinning cone columns to reduce the musts, which has the potential to boost the quality even higher. With the large number of brands on the market, competition should keep prices down.

Here are notes on several of my fermentations.

"SIX-MONTH" ASEPTIC JUICE
23 LITERS OF "BURGUNDY"

LABEL: *23° B. sugar; 3.60 pH; 7.5 grams total acid; 78 parts per million sulfite.* (My hydrometer read 23° also; my Titret® ampule showed something less than 70 ppm sulfite; and the pH of the finished wine was 3.52.)

DAY 1. Began a yeast starter by emptying a package of yeast in $^1/_2$ cup of warm water. Fifteen minutes later, when it was fully hydrated, I added 1 tsp. of sugar and a pinch of diammonium phosphate and set it aside. Poured entire 6 gallons, including pulp and sediment, into 7-gallon carboy rather than using a primary fermenter. Two hours later, I added the yeast starter over the surface of the must and emptied another package of the same yeast (Red Star Premier Cuvee) for good measure.

DAY 2. Fermentation underway. No air lock.

DAY 4. Vigorous fermentation. Sugar down to 1° B.

DAY 5. Hydrometer indicates sugar is -1° B. Still fermenting actively but much slower. Racked from the large carboy into 5-gallon carboy plus 3-liter jug. Topped with air locks.

DAY 11. Fell still.

DAY 14. Racked and sulfited (25 ppm). Final volume was almost 6 U.S. gallons. Set it outside to cold stabilize. After a month in the cool spring air, most of the solids will have settled out and the wine could be bottled. However, it has a sharp "bite" to the palate, as though a large amount of acid was added.

MONTH 2. Racked, adding 3 ounces of sugar to raise the residual sugar level to .5%. The sugar made the wine more mellow but a bit more is needed to balance the acid. Added another $1^1/_2$ ounces of sugar, which seemed to add the desired balance.

MONTH 3. Bottled. The adjustments elevated this wine to what might be considered jug wine quality. The packaging did not indicate what is meant by "Burgundy," but I doubt that it contains any Pinot Noir.

MONTH 8. Quite to my surprise, it aged into a respectable red wine with some Pinot Noir qualities. At .75% RS it is too sweet, which was my error in judgement. For some reason it has a slight caramelized flavor.

"SIX-MONTH" ASEPTIC JUICE

23 LITERS OF "JOHANNISBERG RIESLING"
LABEL: *21.2° B. sugar; 3.00 pH; 8.3 grams total acid; 93 ppm sulfite.*

DAY 1. Poured contents into 7-gal. glass carboy containing Steinberg lees from prior fermentation of Gewurztraminer. Added $1/2$ tsp. DAP. Held overnight at room temperature.

DAY 2. Fermentation underway. Took to garage to cold ferment.

4 WEEKS. Still fermenting, but very slowly. Hydrometer reads negative. Set in warm room to complete fermentation. If the sugar had been higher initially, I might have stopped fermentation at 1% RS. But at 21° B., the alcohol level will only be 11%, so I need not be concerned about high alcohol. It is easier just to add sugar back. Another option for adding a bit of residual sugar after fermentation would be the concentrated conditioners marketed by some of the concentrate kit companies, which is pure grape concentrate (fructose) with potassium sorbate to discourage renewed fermentation.

5 WEEKS. Fermentation is complete. Clinitest reads .1%. Removed the air lock and immediately replaced with a solid rubber stopper, wrapped in plastic wrap to give it a good seal. Set the carboy in the garage to settle for a week or two. There is almost a "gallon" of head space in the carboy, which is filled with almost pure carbon dioxide. It is imperative that the stopper not be removed until racking as air would get in. Even if it is not opened, the wine will not be safe for more than two weeks. It would be safer to sparge the headspace with argon.

6 WEEKS. The gross lees have settled out. Racked and sulfited with $1/8$ tsp. per 5 gallons. Have 5 gal. plus $1/2$ gal. Sealed with rubber stopper and set outside to cold stabilize for a few weeks.

8 WEEKS. No further clearing. TA = .86%. Made Sparkolloid slurry (7 tsp./5 gal. since it was quite cloudy) and racked, adding 17.5 g. of calcium carbonate (to lower TA by .14%). No sulfite. The

wine cleared overnight. Much crystallization, which compacted the Sparkolloid lees.

9 WEEKS. TA = .74% — the carbonate lowered TA by .12% rather than .14%. This is a normal deviation. pH=3.2.

3 MONTHS. Racked, sulfited ($\frac{1}{8}$ tsp.) and added 6 oz. of sugar to raise RS to 1%.

4 MONTHS. Wine is crystal clear. Bottled. This turned out to be a pleasant wine that one would never guess was not made from fresh grapes.

"SiX-WEEK" WiNE KiT
JOHANNISBERG RIESLING

DAY 1. Mixed the bentonite in the blender per directions and put into primary fermenter (10-gal. can). Emptied the 15-liter foil bag into a 6-gallon (U.S.) pail. Rinsed the bag with warm water to dissolve the rest of the concentrate and sugar; added more warm water to fill the pail. Dumped the pail into the primary fermenter and stirred. Sugar tested 21° B., which is just right for a Riesling. Rehydrated the Red Star Premier Cuvee yeast (Prise de Mousse) that came with the kit. After sprinkling the starter solution over the surface, I sprinkled another package of the same yeast in dry form directly onto the surface, for good measure. This wine was fermented at room temperature, but there is no reason it could not have been cold fermented over a longer period of time.

DAY 2. Fermentation underway.

DAY 4. Sugar down to 6° B.

DAY 8. Sugar at 2° B. Racked into a 5-gallon carboy and 1.5 liter jug and topped with air locks, discarding the bentonite and yeast lees. I could have fermented it to dryness at room temperature and added sugar back to sweeten it, but I chose instead to set it outside where the cool spring temperatures would slow down final fermentation.

DAY 14. Clinitest indicates that residual sugar is at 1%. Since this is the minimum level of residual sugar one would want in a wine of this type, I racked and sulfited ($\frac{1}{4}$ tsp.) to stop fermentation. The yield was slightly over 5 gallons, the loss in volume being attributable to the use of bentonite. Left it outside so the gross lees could settle.

DAY 28. Very little clarification to date; the wine still looks viscous. Fined with Sparkolloid slurry at the rate of 1 tsp per gallon. The directions say to add meta, sorbate and isinglass at this stage, but I chose Sparkolloid instead, intending to use the isinglass later if necessary.

MONTH 2. It needs a higher level of residual sugar for good balance. Racked, adding $\frac{1}{8}$ tsp. of sulfite and 6 ounces of table sugar to raise residual sugar from 1% to 2%. This seemed about right for my taste. The wine has cleared noticeably by now, though it will never be brilliant.

MONTH 3. Bottled. This is a pleasant semisweet Riesling. It would not win any awards, but most people would regard it as drinkable, if not enjoyable. I anticipate that it will improve somewhat with six months in the bottle.

MONTH 8. This has developed into a nice Riesling without a trace of the "caramelized" flavor normally associated with a concentrate. The only shortcoming is that it is far too sweet for my palate. I should have left the residual sugar at 1%.

"SIX-WEEK" WINE KIT

ZINFANDEL

DAY 1. Emptied the 15-liter foil bag into a 6-gal. (U.S.) pail. Rinsed the bag with warm water to recover any remaining sugar and filled the pail with warm water. Poured into a 10-gal. primary fermenter and stirred. The pH tested 3.55 and total acid measured .69, which are good numbers. The sugar was low, however, at 18° B. Trusting the producer, I resisted the temptation to add more sugar. As a source of yeast and hopefully some added bouquet, I added approximately 1 gallon of skins of Cabernet Sauvignon (with the seeds shaken out using a nylon hops bag)—I had pressed a batch of Cabernet Sauvignon the same day.

DAY 2. Fermentation started. The cap will be punched down once or twice a day from now on.

DAY 6. Fermentation has come to a near standstill. Dipped the skins out with a stainless steel kitchen strainer and pressed by hand in a coarse nylon hops bag. Transferred the wine to glass containers. Attached air locks stored at room temperature. Have 5 gal. carboy + 1 gal. jug, both almost full.

DAY 9. Almost dry. Residual sugar tests .2% using Clinitest.

DAY 22. Set outside to chill.

5 WEEKS. Racked and sulfited — $\frac{1}{4}$ tsp./ 5 gal. Some tartrate salts have already precipitated. Net yield was 5 gal. + 3 liters. Stored at room temperature for further settling.

10 WEEKS. Bottled. I cheated a little by adding $\frac{1}{2}$ tsp. of my Raspberry Liqueur (*appendix F*) per bottle. TA = .66%. RS = .15%. pH = 3.49. Should be a very drinkable table wine in a few months.

Note: Malolactic fermentation is generally not advised for kits. In most cases the manufacturer will have increased or decreased the amount of malic acid to get the optimum level and balance of acids. In addition, it would be difficult to initiate malolactic fermentation with the relatively high level of sulfite in kits.

Chapter Sixteen

Blending

lending can be very exciting because two well-balanced wines having no defects can often be blended solely for the purpose of getting a better wine. You can start with wines that are good to great and with the right blend end up with something that is even better! In Europe, the advantage of blending has been recognized for many generations, and it will probably become even more common there as trade barriers fall within the European Common Market. Blending is just beginning to find acceptance in the United States, where straight varietals have been promoted since inception of the premium wine industry several decades ago.

Blending is a complex topic on which there will not be much consensus beyond a few basic considerations. Here are a few of them to get you started down this interesting path. You can add to them as you go!

Blending different varieties

As a general rule, one wants to avoid blending two varieties where each has a distinctive varietal characteristic in its own right. They are likely to compete with each other — stick with varieties that harmonize with each other. Cabernet Sauvignon and Merlot may be the most classic of all blends. A blend of the two will almost always have more complexity and character than either one by itself. The Merlot will soften Cabernet Sauvignon, which is inherently quite tannic and slow to mature. Or, depending on the proportions, the Cabernet Sauvignon will add some backbone and character to Merlot, which the latter usually needs. Other Bordeaux varieties also blend well: Merlot and Cabernet Franc; Cabernet Sauvignon and Cabernet Franc.

The classic Rhone wine is a blend of up to thirteen varieties, including four white wines. Two of the principal red varieties — Syrah and Grenache — blend very well, and the blend can often be improved with a small percentage of Viognier, a white grape with unusual characteristics. The latter emphasizes aroma and extends the after taste.

Blending is by no means limited to the classic Bordeaux or Rhone varieties. Witness the tremendous growth of Cabernet Sauvignon-Syrah and Syrah-Cabernet Sauvignon blends. Syrah has good mouth feel and aromas and shares these qualities nicely with other red varieties.

It may be my impatience, because straight Zinfandel seems to take so long to mature; but I think Zinfandel is improved by the judicious blending of lesser amounts of other varieties, such as Grenache, Carignane or Syrah. As a rule, 5 to 10% of another variety can be blended without diluting the varietal characteristic of the main wine. At levels above 15%, however, the varietal characteristic starts to become less distinct. If you add 25% of Grenache or Syrah to Zinfandel, for instance, the blend will mature faster and be more complex, but will have less Zinfandel character. You benefit in the short run by blending, but after five years in the bottle, the straight Zinfandel might very well show better. There is almost always a trade-off associated with blending.

Similar considerations apply to the blending of white varieties. As a rule, you will get a better result by blending a neutral or semi-distinctive variety with a distinctive one—they harmonize better. Sauvignon Blanc and Semillon are often blended, and either can be blended with Chardonnay, although it is not done with premium Chardonnays. Except in the case of sparkling wines, it is difficult to improve Chardonnay by blending.

I sometimes press a small quantity of Pinot Noir without crushing and use the resulting *blanc de noirs* for blending with other white table wines, such as Sauvignon Blanc and Semillon. Adding 5 to 10% of white Pinot Noir seems to give a Sauvignon Blanc or Semillon more body. When using Pinot Noir in this fashion, you want the varietal characteristic to be low, so grapes with sugar in the range of 19-20° B. should be used. These are the same grapes that one would want for making a sparkling wine. The next time you make a *blanc de noirs* sparkling wine, make a little extra and try some sample blends to see how you like it!

Methodology

Wines to be blended should first be individually evaluated. Which wine do you want to improve and in what way? Is it too dark or too light in color? Is one of them overly fragrant? Do you want a higher fruit profile? Do you want more tannin for a longer "window of drinkability?" Do you want an austere wine? Are you looking for a big bouquet? A lingering aftertaste? It's easy to get confused in the midst of evaluations if you are only trying to decide which blend is "best." Most of the time you will get an outcome more to your liking if you decide beforehand what the goal is. Your attention in this respect is directed to the last section of this chapter. The input of others can be invaluable in defining the goal of the blend, as well as evaluating the final outcomes.

Since there is no universal approach to finding the right blend ratio, you will have to adopt and revise your own technique as you go. I have settled upon four different combinations (80:20, 60:40, 40:60, and 20:80) plus a control of each variety. The controls are a reference in case none of the blends are better than the individual wines — nothing is to be gained by blending unless the result is better.

Some winemakers do more sample blends in finer increments, which is a good practice. I do essentially the same thing later in the second round of blending. I keep the increments rather limited in round one. If 80-20 seems optimum, for instance, I do a second series of 90:10, 85:15, 80:20 again and 75:25, etc. This way I not only confirm my initial impression, but I might find a better blend in the process. If the optimum blend on the second round is not somewhere in the middle of the pack, then I have reason to question my initial impressions. Finding the right blend can be elusive, so it is good practice to confirm the results.

Blending several wines

All that has been said thus far concerns the blending of two wines. What if you want to blend three wines? Theoretically, one would devise a matrix of the various ratios of the three varieties. This quickly escalates into numbers that far exceed my goal in blending! When blending more than two wines, I usually do a master blend of what I regard as the two main wines. For instance, let's assume that I have done my sensory tests and found that 90% Cabernet Sauvignon and 10% Merlot is the optimum combination. Now I want to see if it can be improved with some Cabernet Franc. Instead of doing a sample blend of all possible combinations of the three wines, I adopt the more modest goal of seeing whether I can improve on my 90-10 master blend with small additions of Cabernet Franc, such as 5%, 10% and 15%. As long as the end result is a better wine, I am content. This is not to say that when the third wine is added, some other ratio of the first two might not be better. Let's assume that my master blend of 90% CS-10% M is improved by adding 5% CF. This produces a blend consisting of 5% CF, 86% CS and 9% M. It could very well be, for example, that 85% CS, 5% M and 10% CF would be even better. I am satisfied any time I can improve on the master blend.

Remedial Blending

Blending can be an excellent way to deal with flaws, such as too much or too little acid, residual sugar, sulfite, alcohol, astringency, color, pH and the like. These qualities can be altered by blending wines of either the same or different grape varieties. The astute blender will always do sample blends and attempt to optimize the sensory outcome as well as the readings.

Maybe you have one wine where the total acid is too high and another where it is too low. Blending is an ideal way to correct both problems. Similarly, an excess of residual sugar in one wine can be remedied by blending with another that has too little. Both of these cases can be calculated mathematically.

Let's assume that you have two carboys of dry white table wine, one with total acid (TA) of .8% and one .5%. Obviously, if you wanted to end up with .65% TA, you would blend equal amounts of each. More likely, the acid levels will not fall into such a neat range or you won't want the midpoint. If one wine is .9% TA and the other .45% TA and you have determined that you want to end up with .6% TA, how are the quantities to be calculated? The following formula is the easiest way I have found to calculate quantities. The result is the <u>ratio</u> of the <u>volume</u> of one wine to the other.

$$TA_1 + TA_2\, X = TA_b\, (1 + X)$$

Where:

TA_1 = Total acid wine no. 1

TA_2 = Total acid wine no. 2

TA_b = Desired total acid of blend

X = Ratio by volume of wine no. 2 to wine no. 1

Example. Total acid of wine no. 1 is .9. Total acid of wine no. 2 is .45. You want a blend having total acid of .6

$$TA_1 + TA_2\, X = TA_b\, (1 + X)$$
$$.9 + .45\, X = .6\, (1 + X)$$
$$.9 - .6 + .45\, X = .6 - .6 + .6\, X$$
$$.3 + .45\, X = .6\, X$$
$$.3 + .45\, X - .45\, X = .6\, X - .45\, X$$
$$.3 = .15\, X$$
$$2 = X$$

The result, X, is the ratio of wine no. 2 to wine no. 1. In this case, 2 volumes of wine no. 2 are needed for one volume of wine no. 1 to end up with acidity of .6%. The calculations would be done the same way with one batch having too much residual sugar and another having too little. Just substitute sugar percentages for acid percentages.

Most measurements lend themselves to the above formula, including alcohol, total acid, residual sugar, and parts per million of sulfite. The one notable exception is pH, which is a logarithmic function. If you blend a gallon of pH 3.8 with a gallon of pH 3.4, you will not get 3.6. The pH will be closer to 3.4 than 3.8 because the 3.4 wine will have a disproportionately greater concentration of hydrogen H^+ ions.

Bench trials

As mentioned, rather than arbitrarily deciding that you want total acid of .6%, it is always better to do bench trials first to determine what acid level <u>tastes</u> <u>best</u>. You might think that TA of .6% will be optimum, but why not try some blends slightly above .6% and some slightly below? Bench trials can be particularly helpful when correcting total acid in white wines because residual sugar is another variable that must be taken into consideration.

My suggestion is that the formula be used to identify some sample blends that are likely to be in the ballpark. Use it to determine how many milliliters of one wine versus the other is needed to result in .55% TA. Then do the calculation for .60%, .65%, etc. After calculating the ratios, mix a few milliliters of each at .55%, .60%, .65% and .70%. I use medical syringes from the drug store (or pipets) for blending small volumes because they conveniently measure in milliliters. Once you have decided on a blend, the same ratio will apply to blending in gallons as in milliliters.

Note that blending does not always pay off. If one lot is well balanced and promises to be exceptional, think twice before sacrificing it to salvage a substandard lot. It might be better to keep the promising wine intact and find some other way to deal with the lesser one. For one thing you have to blend a much greater volume of the wine having normal acid or residual sugar to correct one that is significantly outside the desired range. It's just the way the numbers work. In any event, I would certainly do bench tests to make sure that the reserve quality wine will not be unduly compromised by the blending and that the lesser one is sufficiently enhanced. It has to be worth the trade-off.

When to blend

There are three times when blending is most commonly done: 1) before fermentation; 2) shortly after it falls still; and 3) right before bottling. Blending before fermentation would have the advantage of allowing everything to integrate during fermentation but is impractical unless you have cold storage, because grapes will seldom ripen at the same time. And there is an inherent disadvantage in not knowing anything about either of the wines-to-be before the blend. As a result, most blending is done after fermentation.

You could start as early as the first racking. However, the wines will still be very yeasty and astringent. A better assessment can be made by waiting a few more months. Late spring is a good time to get serious about blending because the wine temperature will be higher, the flavors more pronounced and the wines less astringent.

Some who barrel-age their wines like to blend, based on tannins, just before the wine goes into the barrel. This allows the wine tannins to integrate with the wood tannins. However, there can be an advantage in waiting until just before bottling to blend because one of the wines might turn out to be an exquisite, single-vineyard wine that needs no help. You would not know that before barrel aging because the wine would not have developed its individuality yet.

Most of the time I suspect that you will have wines of several different varieties or vineyards and will be trying to "craft" a blend, as discussed early in this chapter. This can best be done late in bulk aging.

Additional considerations

Never blend to correct flaws such as oxidation, acetaldehyde, ethyl acetate or acetification — or you will most likely end up with twice as much troubled wine. Some authorities make an exception for volatile acidity (VA) that is only slightly high, since some VA is said to be desirable. This depends on how high the VA is and your tolerance for it. My tolerance is extremely low, so I would never attempt to dilute detectable VA by blending.

There should be no residual sugar or malic acid remaining in any blending wines that were inoculated with MLF bacteria. Of course, if you are dealing with wines where malolactic fermentation is not desired and they have never been inoculated, this will not be a consideration.

Although oak tannins will mellow over time and are desirable in the background of the finished wine, if you oak before blending, the oak flavor and tannins will mask a lot of the fruit and bouquet. This in my opinion interferes with the evaluations. It works better to concentrate on evaluating the fruit and bouquet and blend to maximize those qualities. Then add the oak.

Sensory evaluation

Each individual wine should be evaluated before being sample blended so that you can decide what changes you want. The blends should also be carefully evaluated. This is where your friends come in! A tasting session is a nice occasion to have friends over and solicit their opinions. Hopefully, they will be experienced wine tasters and be familiar with the varieties at hand. If there is a particular commercial wine that you would emulate, by all means include a bottle in the array.

Taste evaluations should be done in a clean, well-lighted room, away from socializing and odors, such as tobacco or perfume. Each person should have wine glasses of uniform size and shape, and the wines should all be the same temperature. Bread and water are fine to renew the palate, but if you are tasting a large number of samples, don't swallow. Encourage everyone to spit and dump to keep their taste buds alive longer. Have pens and paper available and ask them to give the reasons behind their preferences. I usually do a blind tasting in that no one knows what the blend is. The order could be totally random, but your feedback might be more focused if the blends are arranged in ascending or descending order.

When you are reflecting on all the input, take the consensus of the group into account, but also factor in the differences in their palates. You know what you like and how you want your wine to turn out. Let the final decision be your own!

TESTING PROCEDURES

Testing sugar content

This is the easiest of all tests. All it requires is a hydrometer and cylindrical jar to hold the sample. Take the reading from the bottom of the meniscus (refer to page 20). Note that pulp and solids suspended in the liquid will cause an artificially high reading. If you test right after pressing, deduct $1\frac{1}{2}°$ B. as a rule of thumb. A better reading will result if the test sample is settled overnight and only the clear juice tested the next day. The degrees of sugar in a must is a rough indicator of the potential alcohol level — the actual alcohol level will be roughly 55% of the Brix reading (e.g., 20° B. will result in a wine with 11% alcohol, more or less). A hydrometer will not read the actual alcohol level; a vinometer is required to do that.

The two most common scales for measurement of sugar are Brix and the older Balling scale. The two are essentially the same, except that Brix is standardized at a temperature of 20° C (68° F), whereas Balling is standardized at 15.5° C (59° F). The difference is not significant, so I treat the two scales as equals.

The calibrated temperature is marked on most hydrometers. If the temperature of the must is higher than the calibrated temperature, add approximately .25° B to the reading for each 9° F (5° C); if the actual temperature is below the calibrated temperature, deduct .25° B from the reading for each 9° F (5° C) of difference.

Testing total acid

It's important to know the level of total acid of the must, starting at the time of the crush. Plan to do your own titration test when the grapes arrive, even if the vineyard gave you its reading. Your reading, even if less accurate, is the more important reference point for later measurements of the change in acid level after cold stabilization, during malolactic fermentation or after acid adjustment.

Acid titration tests require minimal equipment and can be purchased in kit form or assembled:

> Small beaker or jar
> .1N or .2N sodium hydroxide
> Distilled water
> Phenolphthalein
> Burette, or a 1 ml pipet, or an eye dropper

My preference is the 1 ml graduated pipet, which is calibrated to .01 ml. A pipet is faster than a burette once you learn to control the rate of discharge. If you have only an eye dropper available, one drop quite consistently equates to .05 ml. For most accurate results, the test sample, hydroxide and pipet or burette should all be at the same temperature. The sample should also be settled to eliminate the pulp. It is easiest to read the color change against a white background, such as sunlight reflected off white paper.

If you have .1N hydroxide, start with 1 ml of sample wine or must; if you have .2N hydroxide, start with a 2 ml of sample. When adding either hydroxide or wine sample, the excess should be wiped off the outside of the pipet so an extra drop does not sneak in. Add the sample to a beaker and then add about an ounce of hot distilled water. Add a couple drops of phenolphthalein. Slowly drip hydroxide from the pipet into the beaker, swirling continuously, until you reach the endpoint, which will be indicated when the phenolphthalein turns faint pink and stays pink for 10 or 15 seconds. Multiply the ml of hydroxide used by .75, and the result is total acid in grams per 100 ml, measured as tartaric. For example, if you started with 2 ml of sample wine or must and used .8 ml of .2N hydroxide, total acidity would be .6 (.8 ml X .75). Note that you would get the same result if you started with a 1 ml sample and used .1N hydroxide; .8 ml of hydroxide would have been used and acidity would be .6%.

A 50-ml burette is more work to set up and clean, but it requires less manual dexterity to use. The only difference in using a burette and 250-ml Erlenmeyer flask is the quantities of sample and hydroxide used. After getting the burette set up and clearing the air out of the channel so the hydroxide will flow freely, add 5 ml of wine or must sample to the beaker using a 5-ml pipet. Add 3 or 4 ounces of hot distilled water and 6 or 8 drops of phenolphthalein. Make note of the level of hydroxide in the burette, measuring from the bottom of the meniscus. Drip hydroxide in and swirl the flask until it turns faint pink and holds for 20 seconds. Measure the new level in the burette, subtract to determine how many milliliters were required and multiply the result by .15. If 7 ml of .1N NaOH was needed to neutralize the 5-ml sample, total acidity is 1.05 (7 X .15). If you used .2N hydroxide, use a factor of .3. Half as much hydroxide would have been required, so you would get the same result of 1.05 (3.5 ml x .3 = 1.05).

In the case of red wines it is difficult to identify the titration endpoint because the phenolphthalein indicator is the same color as the sample. So you have to watch carefully. As the hydroxide is dripped in, the test solution will gradually turn lighter pink, then slightly gray and then almost clear. The endpoint will be indicated when it turns faint pink again and holds for 20 seconds.

Use of a pH meter is the most accurate way to detect the endpoint when titrating red wines. If you are titrating with a pH meter, the endpoint will occur at 8.1 or 8.2 pH, which is the pH of water. Note that the pH meter will not know how you got to the endpoint; if your hydroxide is weak, the reading will still be overstated.

Standardizing sodium hydroxide

Sodium hydroxide loses its strength through exposure to carbon dioxide in the air. The weaker the solution, the faster it deteriorates. The best practice is to divide your 16 ounce bottle into four ounce bottles and use one at a time. This works acceptably well for acid titrations, even though it will be weaker toward the end of the bottle. Be aware that you can also buy ampules of concentrated hydroxides or acids which store well and which will make a solution of exact strength when diluted to 1 liter with distilled water. Again, break it down into small lots and share with fellow winemakers.

My preference is to open a fresh bottle more often and not worry about standardizing. But in a bind, sodium hydroxide can be standardized against a stable acid of known strength, such as hydrochloric acid (HCl) or potassium acid phthalate (KaPh). This allows one to ascertain the exact strength of a hydroxide, and to adjust titration readings accordingly.

PROCEDURE FOR STANDARDIZING 0.1 N NAOH
WITH POTASSIUM ACID PHTHALATE, 0.1 N

Pipet 5 ml of 0.1 N KaPh into a beaker or small glass. Add 3 or 4 drops of phenolphthalein and titrate with your 0.1 N NaOH until it turns faint pink and holds for 20 seconds after stirring. The normality of your hydroxide is determined by this formula:

$$\frac{\textbf{ml of KaPh X Normality KaPh}}{\textbf{ml NaOH}}$$

If 5.2 ml of NaOH were required to neutralize 5 ml of the phthalate, the normality of the hydroxide would be 0.096N:

$$\frac{\textbf{5 ml X 0.1}}{\textbf{5.2}} = \textbf{0.096}$$

A total acid reading, for example, would have to be adjusted downward by multiplying by the factor of 0.96. $\left(\frac{0.096}{0.1}\right)$

PROCEDURE FOR STANDARDIZING
<u>WITH HCl 0.01 N:</u>

When working with very dilute solutions, it is good practice to neutralize some distilled water before the test. Bring about 100 ml of distilled water to a boil, add 5 or 6 drops of phenolphthalein and neutralize with a dilute base until it turns a faint pink and holds. Now add 5 ml of 0.01 N hydrochloric acid and titrate with the subject sodium hydroxide to the same faint pink. Since hydrochloric acid is also a mono-acid, the formula for calculating normality will be the same as for potassium acid phthalate:

<u>ml of acid std. X Normality acid std.</u>
ml of test hydroxide

If it took 4.8 ml of hydroxide, the normality of the hydroxide would be 0.0104.

$$\frac{5 \text{ ml X } 0.01}{4.8} = .0104$$

If you were doing the titration in a vacuum aspiration test, for instance, the reading would have to be increased by a factor of 1.04. ($\frac{0.0104}{0.01}$)

Testing residual sugar

"Clinitest" tablets are a simple and reliable way to measure the level of unfermented sugar left in a wine, commonly referred to as residual sugar, or "RS." They come packaged with two color charts — 0 to 2% RS, and 0 to 5% RS. However, the older "Dextrocheck" chart, if you can find one, is better, as the color patches are on an ideal scale for the testing of dry wines of 0% RS (blue) to 1% RS (orange). This scale is more convenient and accurate for dry wines than the charts packaged with Clinitest kits. Some wine supply shops or distributors have Dextrocheck charts available upon request. The three charts are summarized on the next page.

CHART	RS Range	No. of Drops	Volume
2 drop Clinitest	0–5%	2*	.1 ml
5 drop Clinitest	0–2%	5*	.25 ml
Dextrocheck	0–1%	10	.5 ml
* Plus 10 drops of water			

In addition to Clinitest tablets, you will need a test tube and a $1/2$ ml or 1 ml pipet (or at least an eye dropper). To test using the Dextrocheck chart, drop $1/2$ ml (10 drops) of the sample wine into the bottom of the test tube, drop a Clinitest tablet in and watch the color change from blue to green and possibly to orange as the reaction goes to completion. After the reaction stops, wait a few seconds and compare the color against the chart. Using $1/2$ ml (10 drops) of test solution, dark blue will be zero RS on the Dextrocheck chart and orange will represent 1% RS.

If the reaction continues after the solution turned orange, the sample has more than 1% residual sugar. In that case you will need to dilute a sample and test again. Use .25 ml of sample wine (5 drops) and add .5 ml of water (10 drops) for additional liquid. Read the new result directly off the "5-drop" color chart that comes packaged with Clinitest to get the percentage RS. Or, double the results read off a Dextrocheck chart.

Clinitest tablets have many uses. They will confirm that your wine in the carboys fermented to completion; check before adding sulfite! They can be used to test residual sugar after sugar addition, but you have to wait a few weeks until the sucrose has been converted into fructose and glucose.

Clinitest tablets are indispensable if you want to stop fermentation at a predetermined level, such as 1%, before all sugar ferments. This will keep the alcohol level slightly lower and can be used to advantage where the grapes had excessive sugar that might result in an overly alcoholic wine. For example, if the grapes arrive at 26° Brix, the progress of fermentation can be monitored with Clinitest tablets and fermentation stopped at 1% residual sugar by racking, sulfiting and chilling. The alcohol level will be approximately .55% lower than it would be if fermented to dryness and sugar added back to raise RS to 1%. A slow fermenting yeast must be used in order to determine when to intervene and stop fermentation.

Paper chromatography

Chromatography is an easy way for the home winemaker to determine whether or not malolactic fermentation has gone to completion. Fortunately, chromatography test kits are fairly inexpensive and easy to use. A kit will include the following essentials:

- Whatman paper (#1 or #20) — 8 X 10"
- capillary tubes
- capillary tube holder
- chromatography solvent
- wide mouth jar — 1 gal.
- malic & lactic acid reference solutions (0.3%)
- tartaric and citric acid reference solutions (0.3%) (optional)

The acid reference solutions can be purchased or else prepared by dissolving 300 mg of the acid in 100 ml of water. In addition, you will need a pencil and ruler and a stapler to fasten the paper into a cylinder.

Start by drawing a pencil line along the length of the Whatman paper, 1" from the bottom. Place dots at 1" intervals on the line to mark where the liquids will be spotted. A piece of paper will accommodate 3 acid samples and 7 wine samples marked in this manner. Identify each dot on the line with a pencil — "M" for malic, "L" for lactic, "T" for tartaric, etc. Also identify each wine sample to be spotted on the line and tested.

Now dip a capillary tube in the malic acid reference until it is about half full and touch it lightly to the "M" dot. You only want to release enough liquid to make a $1/4$" circle, so lift it the instant any liquid soaks into the paper. Do the same with the lactic acid reference and each other acid or wine sample, using a separate tube for each. Keep each circle as small as possible because that will result in a more clearly defined result. Replace each capillary tube in its ordered slot in the tube holder so they don't get mixed up.

Let the spots dry, which might take 10 or 15 minutes. Repeat the spotting process about 3 more times in the same places so that

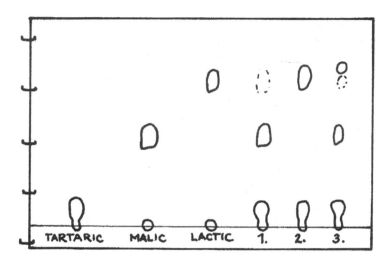

Chromatography Paper Test

an intense acid mark is left at each dot on the line. Hopefully, none will be more than 1/4", but there's no need to start over if a little too much liquid happens to escape the tube. It's just that the smaller and more concentrated the circles, the easier it will be to interpret the outcome when the paper dries.

Spot the paper four or five times. When the acid spots have dried, shape the paper into a cylinder and fasten it with staples. The edges should not overlap because then the acid spots will not move vertically. The pencil line along the base should line up where it meets.

Now pour about 2 ounces of the chromatography solution into the wide mouth jar. Be careful not to breathe the fumes. Stand the paper cylinder upright in the jar, pencil line at the bottom, and put the lid on. The solvent will gradually travel up the paper. Although nothing will be visible until the paper dries, the solvent takes the acid spots with it as it moves upward. Lactic acid travels most, followed by malic, citric and tartaric, in that order.

Leave the paper in the solution for 6 to 10 hours — until the solution has traveled almost to the top. It will take longer for Whatman #20 than #1. Then remove it and hang it to dry away from all chemical fumes. Spots will start to become visible after 2 or 3 hours of drying and will be quite conspicuous when the paper is completely dried. The Whatman paper becomes blue-green and the acid spots are yellow. The lactic reference acid will be closest to the top and the malic spot right below it. The tartaric reference spot will be nearest the pencil line.

Here's how you interpret the results (*see illustration opposite page*). If the wine has not started malolactic fermentation, it will show only a malic spot at the same height as the malic acid reference spot, and no lactic spot, or a very faint lactic spot (see *sample No. 1*). In the case of *sample No. 2*, the lactic spot higher up with no malic spot indicates that it has gone completely through MLF — i.e., no malic remains, all of it having been converted to lactic. If it has both a lactic spot and a malic spot, then MLF is partially complete (see *sample No. 3*). In the latter case, if the malic spot is bold and the lactic spot much lighter, then MLF is just underway, or maybe hasn't even started. If the lactic spot is bold and malic spot faint, then MLF is nearly complete. In this limited sense, the test is quantitative.

The chromatography solution can be poured back into the bottle after the test and reused. The solvent will last a year or more. When the paper turns orange rather than blue-green, the solvent is getting weak. Wash and dry your hands before handling the paper. Store the paper away from chemical fumes.

Note that if any artificial malic acid was added to the wine, as by using an acid blend, a malic spot will always appear. That's because artificial malic acid has a different chemical makeup from natural malic, and only half of the artificial version will be converted to lactic. Some malic will always remain, so chromatography is not a valid test.

Titrets for free SO$_2$

At the levels discussed throughout this book, excess SO$_2$ will not be a problem. But curiosity or a need to know the level of free SO$_2$ could arise. If you purchased pressed juice, it is good procedure to check the level of free SO$_2$ because they may have added more or less than

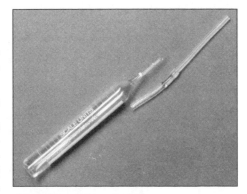

Titret® ampule and slide-on stem.

they thought. (It would also be a good idea to check total SO_2, as discussed below, because some of it binds with the sugar and proteins). Maybe you are having trouble getting malolactic fermentation started and want to know the level of free SO_2. Or maybe you want to adjust free SO_2 at bottling time — red wines should have 20-30 ppm of free SO_2 and white wines 40-50 ppm. The sealed glass ampules marketed by Chemetrics as Titrets® are a convenient way to test free sulfite in dry white table wines that have not been put through malolactic fermentation or been exposed to ascorbic acid. They have good shelf life if kept in the box and not exposed to sunlight. Be aware that they tend to significantly overstate the amount of free sulfite—I always deduct 15ppm from the reading, even for white table wines.

The instructions that come with each package of ten vials are quite good. Push the flexible tube up the slender tippet of the ampule until it reaches the white line. Then gently snap the tippet below that white line. Stick the end in the sample and draw some of the sample up by pinching the glass bead in the flexible tube.

White wines. The ampule will turn dark blue the instant any sample is drawn in and will gradually lighten as more sample is admitted. Titrate until it turns clear, which is the endpoint. Invert the ampule and read the free SO_2 in parts per million.

Red wines. The endpoint is very difficult to detect using Titrets in red wines. As with white wine, the ampule will turn dark blue as soon as wine is admitted. Again, you titrate to the absence of blue. The problem is that the wine will not be clear at the absence of blue; it will be the same shade of red as your original sample. It might help to dilute the sample with an equal part of distilled water (and double the reading), but it is almost as red as before and any error is magnified when you double the reading. It also might help to use side lighting against a yellow background.

The best reference is probably a spent Titret vial filled with some of the original sample. Carefully crunch off the tippet with scissors or pliers so the vial can be drained and refilled with the sample to be tested. A pipet can be used to refill it. When titrating, look for the point where it ceases to become a lighter gray and is the same depth of red as the original sample in the vial. Even then, the readings will vary widely from one person to the next.

Vacuum Aspiration

In addition to the problem of detecting the endpoint in red wines, the Ripper method, including Titrets, has another major shortcoming in that pigments, tannins, acetaldehyde, ascorbic acid, and MLF by-products react with the iodine and cause an artificially high reading. Ripper might read 30 ppm, when in reality you could have as little as 10 ppm. Those who want to closely control the level of free SO_2 will do well to invest in the equipment and chemicals to test by vacuum aspiration, although sending a sample to a lab for analysis always remains an option.

The following equipment and chemicals are needed to test free SO_2 by the vacuum aspiration method, also known as aeration-oxidation. Some of the laboratory supply distributors sell kits containing everything that is needed.

Equipment	Chemicals
Support stand & rod	SO_2 indicator solution
Sidearm flask & clamp	H_3PO_4 Phosphoric acid, 25%
Impinger tube & clamp	NaOH, Sodium hydroxide, 0.01N
#1 stopper with pipet	H_2O_2, Hydrogen peroxide, 30%
#4 stopper with glass rod	HCl, Hydrochloric acid, 0.01N
2.5 watt aquarium pump	Distilled water
Vacuum tubing	Very dilute acid
20 ml volumetric pipet	Very dilute base
Variable-volume dispenser	
(or pipet safety cup)	
1 ml graduated pipet	
100 ml measuring device	

The cost can be reduced by substituting plastic stands to hold the sidearm flask and impinger tube. This eliminates the considerable cost of a stand, rod, and clamps.

Phosphoric acid is added to the wine sample (sidearm flask) to release the SO_2 to a free state. Air is then pushed (or pulled) through the sidearm flask and into the impinger tube, taking the gaseous free SO_2 with it. The SO_2 reacts with hydrogen peroxide in the impinger tube, forming sulfuric acid. The solution in the impinger tube is then titrated with a weak sodium hydroxide to determine the quantity of sulfuric acid. Based on the milliliters of hydroxide required to neutralize the sulfuric acid, the amount of free SO_2 can be calculated. It sounds complex, but after a couple of tests, you will find it to be very easy. Here are the steps:

1. You can use an aspirator pump connected to a faucet to pull air through the sidearm flask and into the impinger. I prefer an aquarium pump to push the air, but the two are functional equivalents.

2. Prepare 100 ml of 1% H_2O_2 by dispensing 3 ml of 30% H_2O_2 into a graduated cylinder and adding distilled water to bring the total volume to 100 ml. This solution will keep overnight if refrigerated but otherwise should be prepared fresh for each testing session. Fill the impinger tube to the 10 ml line with the 1% H_2O_2 and add 2 or 3 drops of indicator solution. This should give it a blue-gray color. If it is aqua, add a drop or two of very dilute acid. If it is purple, add a drop or two of dilute base until it becomes blue-gray. Insert the stopper. Be sure that the tip of the glass rod is below the level of the liquid.

3. Now dispense 20ml of wine sample into the sidearm flask. Then add 20 ml of phosphoric acid (25%) into the sidearm flask —

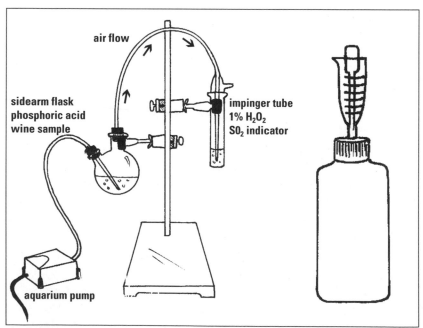

Left: Vacuum aspiration apparatus with aquarium pump. *Right:* Variable-volume dispenser for measuring corrosive liquids.

this lowers the pH and releases the SO_2. If you do not have a variable-volume dispenser to measure the phosphoric acid and are using a pipet instead, be sure to use a pipet safety cup as THIS ACID IS CORROSIVE. Don't ever get it in your mouth. Immediately stopper the flask to retain the gas. Again, the tip of the pipet must be submerged so that air will bubble through the wine-phosphoric acid solution. All the fittings should be tight as the reading will be low if gas is escaping.

4. Turn on the aquarium pump or aspirator and let air bubble through the setup for ten minutes. The solution in the impinger tube should turn purple after a minute or two; if it does not, there is no free SO_2 in the wine, and you can stop the test. If it does turn purple, stop the pump after ten minutes and remove the impinger insert, being certain to allow all the condensed liquid to drip back into the impinger.

5. Titrate the solution in the impinger tube with NaOH .01N until it turns approximately the same shade of blue-gray as it was before aspiration was started. (This point is neither as critical nor as difficult to detect as it is in the case of Ripper with red wines). A 2ml graduated pipet works very well for this titration.

6. Calculate free SO_2 in parts per million as follows:

Free SO_2 (ppm) = 1600 X ml of NaOH used X Normality of NaOH.

If your NaOH was exactly .01N, the formula becomes:

Free SO_2 (ppm) = 16 X ml of NaOH used

You can prepare .01N NaOH by mixing 10 ml of 0.1N sodium hydroxide and 90 ml of distilled water. I always have 0.1N sodium hydroxide on hand because that is the strength I use for acid titration. (Alternatively, glass ampules of most chemicals can be purchased from chemical supply companies referenced in *appendix G* and diluted to 1 liter for a solution with very accurate strength.)Note that hydroxide of such diluted strength as 0.01N is particularly vulnerable to carbon dioxide when exposed to air. It should be kept tightly stoppered and standardized if stored more than a day or two (see *Standardizing sodium hydroxide,* p.163). I find it easier to mix a fresh solution than to standardize.

The indicator solution, which is light-sensitive and should be stored in darkness, has a shelf life of approximately six months.

Testing free SO₂ by Ripper

Vacuum aspiration is the most accurate way to measure free SO_2, but it is also slow relative to the Ripper method. To get the best of both worlds, wineries having many dozens of barrels to monitor often test by both methods initially and make note of the difference between the two — Ripper will always read higher due to the interferences of pigments, aldehydes, *botrytis*, ascorbic acid, etc. Since the difference remains relatively constant, the more efficient Ripper method can be used during bulk aging by subtracting the known overstatement from the Ripper reading. Vacuum aspiration can be used again shortly before bottling to get an accurate reading.

The home winemaker will not have very many specimens to test, so the additional time required to run vacuum aspiration tests will not be a major consideration. The cost could be, however, as it costs two or three times as much for equipment and chemicals as for Ripper.

The following equipment and chemicals are needed to test by the Ripper method:

Equipment
250 ml Erlenmeyer flask
5 ml disposable medicine syringes (for sulfuric acid)
20 ml pipet
10 ml burette
10 ml pipet

Chemicals
25% sulfuric acid—CORROSIVE!! Use syringe or pipet safety cup.
1% or 2% starch indicator
0.02 N iodine solution (store in total darkness)
0.02 N sodium thiosulfate soln. (store refrigerated)
dilute acid and dilute base

Procedure for testing free sulfite:
1. Pipet 20 ml of wine into the flask.
2. Add 2 - 3 ml of starch indicator solution and approximately 5 ml of sulfuric acid using a disposable medicinal syringe.
3. Quickly titrate to a bluish endpoint with 0.02 N iodine solu-

tion — the color should hold for 30 seconds. Don't add the sulfuric acid until you are all set to titrate. Test samples one at a time.

TITRATING FORMULA:

$$\frac{\text{(ml iodine used)} \times \text{(N of iodine)} \times 32000}{\text{ml of wine sample}}$$

Example: 3.9 ml of our iodine solution was required to titrate 20 ml of wine sample. Free $SO_2 = 125$. $3.9 \times 0.02 \times 32000/20 = 125$. However, iodine loses strength and should be standardized frequently.

Procedure for standardizing iodine

Iodine starts to deteriorate instantly if exposed to direct sunlight, less quickly under less intense light. Since a very dilute solution is being used, it should be calibrated frequently, preferably before each testing session and the final SO_2 reading adjusted accordingly.

Pipet 10 ml of iodine to a 50 ml Erlenmeyer flask or beaker. Titrate with .02N sodium thiosulfate until the brownish color is almost gone. Then add 2 -3 ml of starch solution, which will turn it blue. Continue titrating with thiosulfate until it turns clear and holds. Calculate the total volume of thiosulfate used.

Standardizing Formula: The following formula will give you a factor (F), which can be applied to all SO_2 readings for that particular day. N = normality; ml = volume used in milliliters.

$$\frac{\text{(N of thiosulfate)} \times \text{(ml of thiosulfate)}}{\text{(assumed N of iodine)} \times \text{(ml of iodine used)}}$$

Example: 6.5 ml of 0.02N thiosulfate was required to titrate 10 ml of iodine having an assumed normality of 0.02. F = 0.65. This iodine has lost strength; rather than being 0.02 N, it is only 65% of that strength. The factor of 0.65 must be applied to all free sulfite tests run today. In the above example, free sulfite would only be 81 ppm (0.65×125).

Testing total sulfite by Ripper

Total sulfite is a lesser consideration in winemaking in that nothing can be done to lower it after the fact. It should be kept as low as possible, however, by never adding more than necessary because at higher levels it will inhibit malolactic fermentation and bind up some of the esters, which will reduce the wine's bouquet. This is true even if all of it is bound and none free. Since it takes considerable additional equipment to test total sulfite by vacuum aspiration, the Ripper method is most commonly used. A strong base must be added before the test to unbind the bound portion.

1. Pipet 20 ml of wine into the flask. **Add 10 ml of 1N sodium hydroxide (CORROSIVE—use medicinal syringe or pipet safety cup), mix, and wait 10 minutes.**

2. Add a few drops of starch indicator solution and 5 ml of sulfuric acid using a medicinal syringe.

3. Quickly titrate to a bluish endpoint with 0.02 N iodine solution — the color should hold for 30 seconds.

Except for the sodium hydroxide and 10-minute wait, everything else is the same for total sulfite as free sulfite, including the formula above.

If your starch solution becomes moldy, you can make a new solution by mixing 20-25 grams of ordinary starch into 500 ml of distilled water and boiling for several minutes. The commercial products contain a mold inhibitor.

Digital pH meters

A pH meter is extremely useful in gauging the health of a wine. It is a tool that you will want to get if winemaking becomes a serious hobby. Several makes of digital pH meters are available that are both accurate and affordable — $100 to $150 U.S. The Corning pH 40, Piccolo Model 1290 by Hannah and the Oakton pH Testr No. 3 all read to +/- .01 pH and are accurate to +/- .02 pH. I have no doubt that other comparable brands exist. The Corning and Piccolo have a replaceable elec-

Oakton pH Testr 3.

trode so that when it wears out, you can buy an new electrode without having to replace the whole meter. These companies also have models with a BNC connector and cable, which is

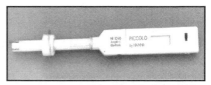

Piccolo Model 1290.

worth the extra cost in my opinion. They also have less expensive models that are only accurate to +/- .1 pH, which will suffice for winemaking if price is a consideration.

You will also need to get small bottles of pH 7 buffer, pH 4 buffer and electrode storage solution. A pH 10 buffer is not a necessity for testing wines, even if you use the meter for identifying the endpoint in acid titrations (pH 8.1-8.2). Get your distilled water at the supermarket.

CONDITIONING A NEW METER. A new meter needs to be conditioned before its first use. Follow the manufacturer's instructions, which are likely to recommend soaking the electrode in storage or buffer solution for an hour or two.

CALIBRATING. A pH meter must be calibrated and the slope set before each testing session. First, soak the electrode in pH 7 buffer for about 10 minutes to hydrate it. The meter does not need to be turned "on" while soaking. After about ten minutes of soaking, turn it on and push the "Standardize" or "Calibrate" button. The digital reading should stabilize in a minute or two. Then push the "Confirm" or "Hold/Confirm" button, and the meter will set itself to read 7.00. This is the point where the concentration of free hydrogen H^+ ions exactly equals that of the hydroxyl OH^- ions and there is zero conductivity

Note that if your buffer became contaminated, as could happen if you poured used buffer back into the bottle to economize, the actual pH will be something other than 7.00. The meter will not know the difference, will set itself to read 7.00 even though the actual pH of your buffer is more or less than 7.00. Your readings will not be accurate, and the inaccuracy could be magnified in the pH 3-4 range of wines and musts. Always discard used buffer solution.

Most meters automatically compensate for the difference in conductivity between the sample temperatures and 25° C (77° F). If your meter does not have automatic temperature compensation, adjust the meter's temperature setting to correspond with the actual temperatures of the buffers and wine or must samples. Then calibrate to pH 7 as described above. Automatic temperature compensation is fine, but to minimize reliance on it, bring your samples in from the cellar and let everything warm to narrow the temperature spread.

SETTING THE SLOPE. After being calibrated to pH 7, the slope must be set. That is, the meter must be instructed that "this is pH 4.00." After rinsing the electrode with distilled water, hold it in pH 4.00 buffer until the digital readout stabilizes. Then push the Calibrate button again. The meter's minicomputer is now able to calculate the slope between pH 7 and pH 4 and points above and below.

Most contemporary digital pH meters automatically calibrate to pH 7.00, pH 10.00 and pH 4.00. All you have to do is to submerge the electrode in the buffer, wait until the reading stabilizes and push the Calibrate or Standardize button. The meter will set itself according to the buffer being used. However, some meters, such as the Piccolo 1290, have a manual set screw. If so, turn the set screw with a jeweler's screwdriver until it reads 7.00, 4.01, 3.00 or whatever known pH you are calibrating to.

To test for accuracy, I keep a buffer of pH 3.00 on hand. You could also use a fully saturated solution of potassium bitartrate (cream of tartar from the grocery store), which has pH of 3.56. Just mix a teaspoon or so of potassium bitartrate in 4 ounces of distilled water and shake it well to dissolve as much as possible. As long as some undissolved white powder remains on the bottom, you know the solution is saturated. If the meter reads close to pH 3.56 and/or 3.00, you are ready to measure the pH of your samples.

TESTING. The actual testing is easy — just submerge the electrode, wait for the reading to stabilize and note the reading.

RINSING. As mentioned, any and all contaminants should be rinsed off the electrode before it is used for the next test or stored.

STORAGE. The electrode should be kept wet during storage to prolong its life. Some meters, such as the Piccolo 1290, have a watertight cap over the electrode, which makes this easy. My Oakton pH Tester No. 3 has no such reservoir, so I wet a tiny piece of tissue to fit over the bulb, wet it with storage solution and store the meter upright. Always use a storage solution (KCl) or a buffer solution for storage. Never use distilled water.

CLEANING THE ELECTRODE. The electrode will eventually become coated with tartrates and pigments, particularly if you test a lot of red wines. If you can see a film or coating on the electrode, hold it under running tap water for a couple of minutes and then very gently stroke it with a wet Q-Tip. The electrode is very fragile, so use only the slightest pressure. Rinse it again in running water and finally soak it in a dilute hydrochloric acid solution (0.01 N). If you don't have hydrochloric acid on hand, use storage solution or pH 4 buffer solution.

PROBLEMS. If the readings are not consistent and drift around, you may only need new batteries or to clean the electrode. Eventually the electrode will wear out and have to be replaced. The manufacturers advise not to expect more than about two years out of an electrode. However, wines are not very corrosive and with proper care a digital pH meter might last for three years. If the electrode is clean and batteries are fresh and the readings jump around or it will not calibrate, chances are that the electrode is worn out. Particularly if you can see tiny air bubbles in the electrode. If so, it's time to replace the electrode or buy a new meter.

Bench trials

Bench trials are almost always advisable before adding a chemical or fining agent to your wine or must, and in some situations bench trials are critical. I normally don't bother with bench trials when fining with bentonite or isinglass since they function independently of each other and are so benign. In the case of tartaric acid and calcium carbonate, I try to avoid formal bench trials by making the additions in small increments when I rack, taking note of the result and using that as a basis for the addition at the next racking. If I need to raise the acid by .1%, for example, I add enough to raise it by .05% and run a titration test before the next racking to see what actually happened. Then I make another small correction when I rack again. This approach, of course, does not work well when lowering acidity with potassium carbonate because you won't know the full effect of the addition until the wine has been cold stabilized. So I add about 80% of the calculated amount and fine tune the acid after cold stabilization with a bit of calcium carbonate (or tartaric acid if I over corrected). With these exceptions,

I run bench trials before treating the main batch of wine.

The goal of a bench trial is to find the minimum addition that will produce the maximum benefit, whether the objective is increasing clarity, reducing astringency or bitterness, or correcting an organic flaw of some type. This is done by methodically adding the chemical or fining agent at different rates to small samples of the subject wine or must and evaluating the result. Once the optimum rate has been determined, you can apply it to the entire batch. The more wine you are fermenting and the better the quality of the grapes, the easier it will be to justify the investment in equipment.

Here is an example of a very simple bench trial. After crushing and pressing some white grapes, it was obvious that the acid was low. I blended tartaric acid and malic acid in equal parts. I drew out one gallon of must and added 1 tsp. of tartaric-malic blend. After running a titration test, I added another 1/2 tsp. of the blended acid to the same gallon of must and took another measurement, etc. As it turned out, another 1/4 tsp. raised total acid to approximately .7%, which was what I wanted. Since I had 15 gallons of must, I knew that I needed approximately 24 more teaspoons for the remaining 14 gallons (14 X 1.75). It was a simple matter of dissolving 12 tsp. of tartaric acid and 12 tsp. of malic acid in the gallon sample and mixing it back into the main batch of wine. This should be done after the solids have settled and the supernatant must has been racked off.

Most of the time the bench trial will have to be more exacting. Here are my suggestions on equipment:

1. 2-Class A graduated pipets, 1-ml. This is the most practical way to run titration tests and to dispense many liquid additives. I often dissolve the needed grams of a chemical in water and dispense it in liquid form with a pipet.

2. Disposable serological pipets, 1-ml. These can be re-used if you remove the cotton wad after the first use, although it is difficult to control the flow. They have a wider tip than the Class A's and are needed for dispensing musts or anything else with solid particulates.

3. A scale capable of weighing to tenths of a gram will be appreciated, but you can usually get by with measuring spoons that

have been checked for accuracy. They vary greatly in volume, even though1 tsp. should be 5 ml.

4. Several one-liter jars, or 100-ml cylinders. I have 5 or 6 plastic hydrometer tubes with the 100-ml, 200 ml, and 250 ml levels marked in permanent ink. This is less expensive than 100-ml graduated glass cylinders.

Conducting bench trials with gelatin-kieselsol or chitosan-kieselsol to clarify a white wine is a much more involved procedure because each is more effective in the presence of the other, but you do not know the optimum rate of either one before starting. But in the case of kieselsol and gelatin, it is known that one liter of 30% kieselsol per 1,000 gallons of wine will be in the ball park and that 2 to 4 ounces of gelatin will be required to counterfine 1,000 gallons of wine (0.15 - 0.30 g. per liter). To work with measurable quantities, 99 ml of distilled water should be added to 1 ml of kieselsol. Shake it well and immediately mix 26 ml of the dilute solution into 1 liter of wine (2.6 ml if you are working with a 100-ml sample). Do this with three different samples, each at the rate of 1 ml per thousand gallons. Shake the samples well to thoroughly mix the kieselsol with the wine.

Wait a few hours and then add the gelatin. Prepare a dilute solution of gelatin by adding 5.6 grams of gelatin to 100 ml of warn distilled water. This would be sufficient for 50 to 100 gallons of wine, so you have to reduce the volume. Add .26 ml to the first 1-liter wine sample, .39 ml to the second 1-liter sample and .52 ml to the third and shake them all for good dispersion. Inspect them the next morning for clarity or taste to evaluate the change in astringency, as the case may be. Pick the best of the three samples and run the numbers for the main batch of wine. If the container is bigger than the sample, I usually give it a puff of argon and cap the container to minimize air contact, but that's not a necessity.

Most home winemakers, the author included, will let it go at that. But a commercial winemaker not wanting to filter might go through the same procedure using .75 liters of kieselsol per thousand gallons and 1.25 liters per thousand gallons. The ratio of gelatin (2-4 ounces per thousand gallons at 1 liter of kieselsol) will stay in the same range. So just decrease gelatin by .75 or increase it by 1.25.

TROUBLE SHOOTING

Difficulty initiating fermentation

If there is no sign of fermentation after 36 hours, something is amiss. If the sulfite was kept within limits, difficulty in initiating fermentation is usually the result of a temperature that is too low. If the must temperature was below 60° F (16° C), the temperature should be raised to 65-70° F (18-21° C). If you cannot raise the room temperature or bring the must inside, you can drop in a couple of plastic milk jugs filled with warm water. Or dip out a couple of buckets of the must, stand them in hot water and dump them back into the fermenter when warmed.

If temperature is not the problem, rack or pour the must into another container, aerating it as much as possible in the process. Or, use a 12-volt electric air pump, hose and racking stem to bubble air through it for a few seconds. Add a teaspoon of diammonium phosphate or yeast nutrient per 5 gallons and sprinkle more yeast on the surface if you are using a dry yeast. Keep the temperature up and it should start.

Stuck fermentation

On rare occasions active fermentation will slow prematurely and eventually stop before all the sugar has been converted to alcohol. This can result from grapes that are deficient in nitrogen, which some vineyards regularly produce. It can also occur after a fermenting must which is nearly dry has been subjected to cold temperatures for an extended period of time. Fermentation will always stop when the temperature drops low enough. And it will always start up again when the temperature is raised. The question is whether it will resume with enough vigor to go to completion. The yeast might not have enough nitrogen stored up to ferment to dryness. It would be a good precaution to add 1 gram of lysozyme per gallon before fermentation to kill all malolactic bacteria as they interfere with some strains of yeast. The lysozyme would also stop the volatile acids from increasing.

If fermentation does not rebound to a healthy rate after the temperature is raised to 70° F (21° C), rack and aerate the wine, adding yeast extract and yeast hulls. Add a teaspoon of balanced yeast food such as Fermaid. It would also be advisable to reinoculate with a fresh starter of a vigorous and alcohol-tolerant yeast, such as Prise de Mousse and to maintain room temperature. Wyeast's Eau de Vie (Vintner's Choice) might be even better because it is vigorous and ferments up to 20% alcohol. Don't be tempted to add diammonium phosphate late in fermentation because the yeast can make very little use of it, and it could taint the wine.

If these measures do not work, the only choice left is to build a new yeast starter solution and start "doubling." Get a small volume of fresh grape juice, preferably of the same grape variety. If you have ten gallons of stuck must, for example, two to four quarts of fresh starter should suffice. If you cannot locate the same grape variety, use a compatible variety that would be acceptable for blending. If that is not possible, use two quarts of Thompson seedless grape juice.

The object is to cultivate a new yeast starter with a vigorous and alcohol-tolerant yeast and once it is fermenting actively, to add an equal volume of the stuck must. If you have two quarts of fresh starter solution, add two quarts of the stuck must. When this enhanced volume is fermenting actively, then double it again by adding four quarts of the stuck must. Then double again, etc.

Activate the yeast and begin the starter the night before, using D.A.P. or a balanced yeast food. Start the doubling process the next morning or as soon as the starter is fermenting vigorously. This project should be closely attended so that the time lag from start to finish is minimized. It should be completed in a matter of a day or two. It is important, before each doubling, to wait until fermentation has fully recovered from the previous doubling. Be sure it is fermenting at the maximum rate that conditions will support before the next doubling of volume. By the time of the final doubling, the unfermented sugar will have dropped to a very low level, and the environment will be much less conducive for fermentation.

A stuck fermentation can sometimes be reactivated, but sometimes not. The sooner it is detected and corrective measures taken, the more likely success in restarting fermentation. It is also more difficult to re-initiate fermentation if the wine is almost dry. If these steps are not successful in restoring a vigorous fermentation, start planning what to do with a sweet wine, such as bottling sweet or blending with next year's dry wine.

Hydrogen sulfide

Hydrogen sulfide, or H_2S, smells like rotten eggs and can be the beginning of *major* problems. Hydrogen sulfide is most likely to be encountered with grapes that had excess sulfur on the skins at the time of crushing, although there are other causes too. The sooner the problem is discovered and addressed, the easier it will be to correct and the less the quality of the wine will suffer. If left to run its course, what starts out as hydrogen sulfide will convert into mercaptans, which are harder to deal with, and then into disulfides, which are even more challenging. The chemical remedy for dealing with mercaptans/disulfides in an advanced stage is beyond the scope of this book as it involves qualitative sensory tests using cadmium sulfate, which is highly poisonous, and using ascorbic acid to convert the disulfides back to mercaptans so that copper sulfate will work. The advice that follows assumes the problem has been detected and addressed early on and has not progressed to the disulfide stage.

If H_2S is detected early in fermentation, the fermenting wine should be racked off the lees and pulp immediately and a balanced yeast food or diammonium phosphate added at the rate of 1 tsp per 5 gallons. This may solve the problem. If the smell returns, rack it a second time and a third time, but omit the chemicals. The object of racking is to separate and discard the pulp on the bottom of the carboy as it contains most of the H_2S-generating constituents. If H_2S is not generated until late in fermentation, the D.A.P. probably will not help. But two or three rackings still might take care of the stink.

As soon as Clinitest confirms that fermentation is complete, the wine should be racked off the lees. Extended aging on the lees is an invitation to post-fermentation conversion of hydrogen sulfide compounds into mercaptans. So rack and sulfite soon after the wine has fallen still, even if the odor has disappeared.

Copper should not be added during fermentation, but it is safe and advisable to add a minute amount of copper after fermentation is complete. Add .3 ml (6 drops) of copper sulfate (1% $CuSO_4 \bullet 5H_2O$) per U.S. gallon (.08ml per liter), which will add .2 ppm of copper. **(Caution - be sure you are using 1% solution and not 10%).** Stopper the carboy and set it in a cool place.

As long as the stopper stays seated, the problem is probably under control. If the stopper starts popping out, the hydrogen sulfide compounds are most likely being converted into mercaptans. Promptly rack again, but this time the wine should be racked into an air-free atmosphere if possible — i.e., displace the air with CO_2 or argon before racking. Add another .15 ml of copper sulfate per gallon. If the smell persists, add another .15 ml per gallon. Even with two or three small additions of copper, after the reaction you will end up well under the FDA limit of .2 parts per million residual. If you added more than .4 ppm of copper sulfate, the wine should be fined with bentonite at some later time to strip out any excess.

The odds are high that these measures, taken promptly as needed, will solve the problem. Some of the compounds may have progressed to the mercaptan stage, but none to the disulfide stage. So the rackings and copper addition should deal with it. However, it is a good precaution to bring a small sample to room temperature and smell carefully from time to time during bulk aging.

Off Odors And Flavors

Browning in a finished wine is a sign of oxidation. Excessive exposure to air could have resulted from fermenting too long in an open fermenter before transferring to carboys or from storage in carboys that were not filled to the top. Fining with Polyclar VT (and sulfiting, of course) after the fact might help reduce the browning.

If your wine has a vinegary taste, the flaw is acetic acid. Since some of this volatile acid is always formed during primary fermentation, it will be present in low levels in virtually every wine, and is not objectionable at low levels. However, at higher levels, which vary from one palate to the next, it becomes a flaw. The acetic acid resulting from fermentation will usually not rise to that level. But if the ever-present acetobacter are given enough time in the presence of oxygen, they will convert ethanol into acetic acid and very likely ruin the wine.

If your wine tastes vinegary and exposure to air was not the cause, perhaps the grapes were overripe or had too much bunch rot, or the pH was high and it was fermented too warm. If a must is fermented warm without sulfiting first, spontaneous malolactic fermentation might have started with one of the undesirable strains that generates acetic acid.

As alcohol is oxidized, the first stage is acetaldehyde. Acetaldehyde is present in all wines and at low levels contributes to complexity. At higher levels it will make a wine seem "flabby" or "flaccid;" (i.e., lacking in fruit and varietal characteristic and seemingly sweet). If ethanol is oxidized further, acetic acid will result and finally ethyl acetate. Ethyl acetate is an ester having a most unpleasant odor, like nail polish remover or airplane glue. It is, to me, the vilest of all organic flaws, although I know people who seem not to detect it or be bothered by it. Although acetaldehyde will bind with sulfite, there is no cure for ethyl acetate in even the smallest amount.

Note that for the most part, there is no satisfactory "cure" for any of the organic defects discussed above. Prevention in the form of a proper pre-fermentation acid level (at least .6% TA), sulfite and air avoidance is by far the best remedy. It is natural to think that by blending, the flaw will be diminished. Depending on the problem, it usually does not work that way — normally the blend is just as flawed as the problem wine. If you have one of these organic defects and sufficient volume of wine to make it worth the effort, consult with someone locally who can give you some perspective, as these problems are difficult to diagnose and treat. Or, send a sample to one of the labs listed in *appendix G*. A heavy dose of sulfite (100 ppm) may be the best palliative. After that, you could consider trying to mask some of the defect with oak flavoring or a higher level of residual sugar.

Finished wines that have a "pruney" flavor were usually made from overripe grapes with high sugar, and were fermented too hot. A pruney flavor right after fermentation will diminish with time, but will not always disappear. If your grapes have abnormally high sugar, keep the temperature in the 70s if you can; don't let it rise to the high 80s. Be sure to sort out all raisined and spoiled grapes before crushing.

Excess Astringency

If a wine is left in contact with the seeds too long, it will become excessively astringent due to the tannin and could take years to mellow. The tannin level can be reduced by fining with egg white, isinglass, potassium caseinate or gelatin, all of which are protein-based and attract tannins. Some of these fining agents deal with astringency more effectively and others deal with bitterness.

Generating Carbon Dioxide

Air is the number one enemy of white wines. Even by keeping the number of rackings to an absolute minimum, the wine will suffer some damage from air contact. However, if the number of rackings is kept to a minimum and the wine is bottled young, the loss in quality will be so minimal as to be undetectable. If more than about three rackings become necessary, or if you end up having to rack in the summer or fall when the wine is more mature and delicate, or if you had problems with microbial activity after fermentation finished, it would be good procedure to displace the air in the empty carboy with an inert gas (such as CO_2 or argon), before racking into it.

This is easy for beermakers with a CO_2 tank and regulator — just fill the carboy with gas right before you rack and the gas, being heavier than air, will settle to the bottom and protect the wine as it flows in. Argon would be even better than CO_2. It is more expensive, but you use so little of it that the cost difference is nominal.

Home winemakers without the luxury of a CO_2 tank can accomplish the same result by fermenting corn sugar solely for the purpose of generating CO_2. Here's how: Dissolve the corn sugar at the rate of 20 ounces per gallon of hot water and add a generous amount of D.A.P. or last year's yeast food. Cane or beet sugar could be used instead, but corn sugar will ferment more willingly. Mash some fruit or vegetables to add nutrients for the yeast; even cucumbers, green tomatoes or carrot shavings will work! Use a vigorous yeast strain, such as Prise de Mousse, and you will soon have a "CO_2 pot," as I call it. If you have other wine fermenting in a carboy, you don't even need to bother with sugar water; just channel the CO_2 from the fermenting carboy.

Channel the gas into the new carboy for an hour or two before racking using a $1/2$" vinyl hose attached to a two-piece, straight-tube air lock. Wrap a piece of aluminum foil around the neck of the carboy while the CO_2 is flowing in. Several carboys can be readied in the days before the racking — just add the $1/4$ tsp. of meta-water, displace the air with CO_2 and stopper them until racking day.

Don't feel that you have to always displace air before racking or run out and buy a tank and regulator. It is not necessary to displace the air as long as the number of rackings is minimized. And it is not necessary at the first racking, when the wine is saturated with carbon dioxide and has little capacity to absorb oxygen. Consider it only when the number of rackings becomes excessive or late in the life of the wine. Or after having experienced microbial activity, when exposure to oxygen should be avoided.

Displacing the air is an extra step and it requires an additional supply of empty carboys. But it is an inexpensive way for the home winemaker to minimize oxygen absorption under conditions where the wine might otherwise suffer noticeable loss in quality.

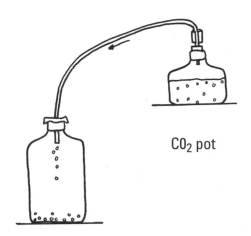

CO$_2$ pot

Grape Varieties

There are hundreds of different grape varieties; the list that follows contains only the more common types, grouped by species.

VITIS VINIFERA

Vitis vinifera is rightfully regarded as the elite species for winemaking. The better ones have no equal. In addition to California and the Pacific Northwest, *vinifera* acreage is increasing in the Northeast and Mid-Atlantic regions of the U.S. and in parts of Canada.

Red vinifera

CABERNET SAUVIGNON. The blue berries of this premier wine grape variety are very small. The resulting high skin-to-juice ratio produces a wine that is very dark, intensely flavored and tannic. Since the skins are tough and the clusters are loose and easily aerated, this variety will survive bad weather before harvest with minimum susceptibility to mildew or bunch rot. Although it takes a fair amount of heat to ripen Cabernet Sauvignon to the point where the wine will have the classic black currant overtones, the grape will grow in cooler climates and produce a respectable red wine. However, if not sufficiently ripened, or if the canopy is so heavy as to restrict aeration and sunlight, the wine will have a vegetative bouquet and flavor. Cabernet Sauvignon buds later than Merlot and is less vulnerable to late spring frosts. The juice is clear when first pressed and makes a wonderful rosé — if you can bear to part with a full-bodied wine! It blends well with Merlot, Cabernet Franc and Syrah.

MERLOT. The plump black grapes of Merlot make a soft, fruity wine very deserving of its current boom in popularity. Merlot is lower in acid, ripens about a week earlier and ages faster than Cabernet Sauvignon. It also tolerates cool, damp soils better than Cabernet Sauvignon, but its thin-skinned berries are more subject to mildew and rot. When Merlot and Cabernet Sauvignon are blended, the result is often better than either one alone. The crop set is erratic and is adversely affected by spring rains right after budding.

CABERNET FRANC. This very cold-hardy red grape does very well in parts of the Northeast United States, Long Island and Ontario's Niagara peninsula, as well as the West Coast. Like Merlot, Cabernet Franc is lighter in color and tannin and ripens earlier than Cabernet Sauvignon. It has traditionally been used in Bordeaux for blending with Cabernet Sauvignon and is gaining in popularity in the United States, both as a straight varietal and for blending. It also blends very well with Merlot. Cabernet Franc tends to overproduce unless the yield is restricted.

PINOT NOIR. Pinot Noir is the most difficult variety to grow and to ferment. Almost never do the results equal the fine red Burgundies by which Pinot Noir wines are inevitably judged. However, with ripe grapes, a very good red wine can be expected. The grape is inherently low in tannin and light in color, and the color diminishes further as the wine ages and bottle sediment develops.

For a lighter wine that emphasizes the grape's delightful fruitiness, try "cold-soaking" for several days after crushing, but before fermentation. This is widely believed to produce a wine with softer flavors, more fruit and a deeper, more stable color. You could also ferment 10-20% whole clusters in the must to emphasize the fruit. By pressing early, say at 5° B, you would avoid the harsher tannins that would be extracted at higher alcohol levels.

For a bigger bodied wine that will take longer to age and have less fruit, but more complexity, crush and de-stem rigorously to macerate the grapes as much as possible. With fully ripe grapes, ten per cent of the stems could be returned to the must before primary fermentation to increase tannin. It could also be put through extended maceration, but this will further reduce the fruit in the wine and is generally not done.

It is usually necessary to put Pinot Noir through malolactic fermentation as a means of getting total acidity down into the desired range. I like a limited exposure to toasted oak; it improves this wine in my opinion.

The many clones of Pinot Noir all tend to have tight clusters and tender skin, which makes them susceptible to mildew and bunch rot if damp weather sets in just before harvest. To hedge against this possibility, you might want to pick some at 18 - 20° B, as Pinot Noir makes an excellent sparkling wine. Press without crushing first, and the juice will be white. This juice is excellent for blending with white wines, such as Semillon, Sauvignon Blanc, and Chardonnay

SYRAH, a.k.a, Shiraz. Serious California wineries are starting to bottle Syrahs that rival the fine wines of Hermitage and Côte-Rôtie, albeit with more fruit and lower tannin. At its best, Syrah makes a big, spicy and complex red wine that takes many years to mellow. It blends well with other red varieties, including Cabernet Sauvignon, Merlot, and Grenache.

ZINFANDEL. When the yield per acre is limited, Zinfandel makes a spectacular, spicy full-bodied wine. "White Zinfandel," so popular with the American public, is fermented from heavily-cropped central valley grapes. Serious winemakers will want grapes originating farther north in California, where cooler weather will allow for slower, more even ripening. When fermenting over-ripe Zinfandel, be sure to cull out those that are raisined and carefully monitor the fermentation temperature to avoid a "pruney" flavor. Try to keep the wine temperature below 80° F. during fermentation. It's okay to leave around .5% of residual sugar in this red wine, as the commercial wineries often do.

White vinifera

CHARDONNAY. It should come as no surprise that the grape that gives us the great Meursaults and Montrachets of Burgundy is so widely planted throughout the world. It is quite hardy and adapts to a wide range of climates. The problem with Chardonnay is that it is a challenge to grow and a challenge to ferment. Unless well ripened, it has little inherent varietal characteristic. The quality of the wine falls off rapidly as the tonnage surpasses the optimum yield per acre, which will vary from one region to the next. Its tight clusters are not easily aerated, making it quite susceptible to mildew and bunch rot in damp weather.

It is best, in my opinion, to soak Chardonnay grapes on the skins for 24 hours before pressing and fermenting. I am partial to cold fermentation with Steinberg yeast, but wineries typically ferment with more vigorous yeast strains at 65° F (or start lower and let the temperature rise after the sugar drops below 10° B). Although I confess to liking the buttery flavor that results from malolactic fermentation, I have mixed emotions about MLF because it eliminates so much of the fruit flavor. It also seems to make the wine more difficult to clarify. When I do opt for MLF, which is usually when total acidity is high, I keep the temperature fairly warm and stir the lees two or three times a week. This imparts the maximum yeasty flavor in addition to promoting MLF. (Note that if you want to keep the temperature abnormally warm during MLF, avoid the vigorous yeasts; otherwise, autolysis is likely, where the yeast cannibalize each other after the sugar is gone and leave a bad flavor). Sometimes, I flavor a Chardonnay with French oak and sometimes not, since the oak flavoring masks some of the fruitiness.

SAUVIGNON BLANC. The vines of Sauvignon Blanc are very vigorous and if not pruned to give the grapes some air and sunlight, the grapes will develop an overwhelming grassy quality. Going to the opposite extreme, many U.S. wineries maximize exposure to air and sunlight by canopy management and put the wine through malolactic fermentation as well. The resulting wine will more easily pass for a Chardonnay than a classic Sauvignon Blanc that goes so well with seafood. Sauvignon Blanc is often blended with Semillon and marketed as "Fumé Blanc."

SEMILLON. Semillon is one of the most widely planted white grapes in the world. It is the basic grape of white Bordeaux and of Sauternes (it is very prone to *Botrytis cinerea*, the "noble rot"). Semillon is commonly blended with Sauvignon Blanc to round out the flavor of the latter and with inexpensive Chardonnays as an extender. With the right grapes, Semillon will make a serious white wine capable of long-term aging.

PINOT GRIS. This relative of Pinot Noir is known as Tokay in Alsace and as Pinot Grigio in Italy, where it produces an excellent, dry white wine with a pleasing lemony quality. In the United States it can make a high quality white wine rivaling Chardonnay or Sauvignon Blanc in quality. If well ripened, Pinot Gris wines have a pleasant spicy quality; but if allowed to get overripe, the grapes tend to lose character and will turn red if left to hang too long. Pinot Gris tends to have high acid and low pH, even at high sugar levels. Malolactic fermentation can often be used to good advantage, to add some body to the wine. Pinot Gris is less susceptible to mildew and bunch rot and ripens earlier than Chardonnay.

JOHANNISBERG RIESLING, a.k.a, White Riesling. This is a great one for home winemakers to ferment! It is more widely available than other varieties because the vines are very hardy and will thrive in cooler climates, such as the northeast United States and southeast Canada. It does extremely well in New York. Even if it is harvested early and sugar is added, Riesling will make a nice wine with a distinctive aroma. It can be made dry or sweet or in between and is a good grape for sparkling wine. Riesling can be left hanging longer than other varieties because the berries are highly resistant to frost. If healthy grapes are left to hang, with luck they might become infected with *Botrytis cinerea*, and you will have the makings for a delicious sweet wine! (Note that in hot climates Riesling ripens too quickly and loses much of its quality).

GEWURZTRAMINER. I have never figured out why Gewurztraminer lacks commercial appeal because they can be such fine wines — perhaps the majority of the buying public have never had a good one. Gewurztraminer is similar to Riesling in that it excels in cool climates and makes a good dry wine as well as sweet. The berries are small and pink and the wine is full-bodied, aromatic and easy to recognize. The acid level tends to fall rapidly as Gewurztraminer ripens, so tartaric acid often must be used to raise acidity. The wine sometimes has a slightly bitter aftertaste. Fining with gelatin/kieselsol or isinglass might help deal with that tendency.

FRENCH HYBRIDS

There are dozens of different French hybrids, interspecific hybrids and French-native American hybrids under cultivation in the Midwest, Southeast, Northeast regions of the United States and in parts of Canada. They generally were selected over *vitis vinifera* varieties for their greater cold hardiness, tolerance of humidity, and/or resistance to fungal diseases, rot, pests and mildew. They are superior to *vitis labrusca* because they are less foxy and make far better wines. However, if allowed to over-ripen, some hybrids will develop a "cotton candy" and foxy flavor. It is critical that they be harvested at the right level of ripeness. Commercial wineries often deal with these unwanted flavors by heat treatment and/or carbonic maceration. Avoid extensive skin contact during fermentation of red hybrids and plan to press as soon as the wine has developed sufficient color.

Hybrids for the most part are diminishing in importance as more is learned about cultivating *vinifera* varieties in different locales. The white hybrids are generally of higher quality than the reds.

Following is a list of the better hybrids for winemaking.

White French hybrids

CAYUGA WHITE. Cayuga White is a relatively new cross which is productive, disease-resistant and very versatile. It can be fermented into a fruity, off-dry white wine or, with oak aging, into a more complex, dry table wine. It's also good for sparkling wine. Don't let it get too ripe or it will develop some foxiness.

VIDAL BLANC, a.k.a Vidal. With fully ripened grapes Vidal blanc will make a good fruity, floral wine reminiscent of Riesling — dry, semisweet or sweet. It is popular in Canada as a late-harvest dessert wine. It is a heavy producer and needs a long growing season, so cluster thinning is required.

SEYVAL BLANC. This is a good white hybrid of long standing. It ripens early and can be fermented in various styles — crisp, dry, fruity or put through MLF for a more complex wine. Seyval Blanc is productive and does well in cool climates, but it is very susceptible to bunch rot.

VIGNOLES, a.k.a Ravat. Vignoles ripens to a high sugar level while retaining high acidity, making it an excellent choice for late-harvest and ice wines. It can also be made into a dry white table wine. In addition to its versatility, Vignoles is a very hardy and is seldom affected by frosts since it has a late budbreak. Its principal drawback is that very compact clusters make it highly susceptible to bunch rot.

TRAMINETTE. This is a new variety developed at the NYS Agricultural Experimental Station by Cornell University. According to all reports, it should not be stigmatized as a "hybrid." It is just starting to become commercially available and is expected to establish itself quickly because the wine, similar to Gewurztraminer, is high quality, has a good balance of sugar, acid and pH, and ages well. The vines are cold hardy and the berries quite resistant to rot and mildew.

Red French hybrids

CHAMBOURCIN. This is a relatively new hybrid that makes a full-bodied wine of good quality when the grapes ripen fully. The wine is fruity and aromatic, slightly herbaceous. Due to high yields per acre, it should be cluster thinned. Chambourcin will tolerate humidity and is cold hardy. It ripens mid-season.

CHANCELLOR, a.k.a Seibel 7053. Though not quite as well regarded as Chambourcin, this transplant from the Rhone Valley makes good reds and rosés. It is moderately hardy. Clusters should be thinned to promote ripening. It is susceptible to mildew.

BACO NOIR, a.k.a Baco No. 1. Makes an intense red wine with some aging potential, despite low tannin. It is very vigorous, but disease-prone and frost-prone due to early budbreak.

MARECHAL FOCH, a.k.a Foch. This winter-hardy hybrid has been around a long time. It ripens very early and its black berries produce a fruity red wine with some Burgundian qualities. It lends itself to carbonic maceration.

VITIS LABRUSCA

The wines made from *vitis labrusca* tend to have a "foxy" quality which experienced wine drinkers find objectionable. The riper the grape, the more pronounced the foxiness; so with these varieties, it is better to harvest a little too green than too ripe. However, if picked green they will be quite acidic. As a result, 3 or 4 parts of the must is commonly diluted with one part of water sweetened to about 20° B with table sugar. Foxiness is also reduced by pressing immediately after crushing to minimize skin contact. It's a good idea to line the press basket with fiberglass mesh as the tough slipskins make pressing difficult. Pressing is made easier and the yield increased if pectic enzyme is used.

DELAWARE. The small pink berries of Delaware ripen early and are used to make sparkling wines in particular, but also dry, sweet and ice wines. It has a spicy, musky aroma and is probably the least foxy *labrusca*.

CATAWBA. Since it is quite foxy, these pink grapes are usually converted into white or pink dessert wines, of which the quality can be quite good. It is also used for super-sweet ice wines. The grapes are acidic and the wine will improve somewhat with age. It requires a long growing season.

NIAGARA. This white grape is quite foxy and aromatic. It is usually used to make a sweet version, but sometimes dry. The vines are vigorous and productive.

CONCORD. This is probably the least desirable *labrusca*, due to foxiness and harshness. It has high acid and is best made into a sweet wine.

Fermentation Notes

CABERNET SAUVIGNON

MALOLACTIC FERMENTATION

Extended Maceration

DAY 1. Crushed and destemmed 130# Cabernet Sauvignon. Tested 25° B. right after pressing, with pulp (probably about 24° B. without pulp); .83 TA; 3.43 pH. Sulfited @ $1/4$ tsp./5 gal. of volume; used pectic enzyme to hasten maceration. Added 1 tsp. of diammonium phosphate. Soaked overnight on skins. Grapes had little flavor.

DAY 2. Brought into warm room — used space heater to raise ambient temperature to 75-80° F (24-27° C). Inoculated with Pasteur Red starter solution sprinkled over surface. Fermentation was visible in a few hours.

DAY 3. Cap starts forming.

DAY 4. Deep cap. Since malolactic fermentation is desired with the acid being .83, this is the time to add ML starter & yeast extract. Note that it is normal for the temperature of a fermenting wine to run 5-15° F (3-8° C) above ambient temperature. This is due to the heat generated by fermentation. You want the fermenting wine temperature to run up to 80-90° F (27-32° C) for two or three days during active fermentation in order to maximize extraction of flavors and color. Monitor with a floating thermometer or an indoor-outdoor digital thermometer and don't let it exceed 90° (32° C). Wine must be punched down at least twice a day.

DAY 10. Cap is greatly diminished. Unfermented sugar is slightly over 1%, per Clinitest. Room temperature and wine temperature are almost the same now at 75° F (24° C). It could be pressed now, but I am putting this batch through extended maceration. Covered the cap with a layer of plastic wrap after punching down, to keep air away.

DAY 11. Punching down once a day now and covering with plastic wrap.

DAY 14. Wine is dry. Clinitest turns slightly yellow, but the red pigment is so overwhelming that a reliable reading on residual sugar is not possible. Hopefully, the slight bubble formation is a sign of malolactic fermentation, but it might just be trapped CO_2 escaping. Tastes bitter and tannic.

DAY 16. Still some bubbles escaping. Cap floating on surface, so no need to punch down. Wine mellowed; has spectacular flavor and fruit — should be excellent wine!

DAY 17. Wine bitter again.

DAY 20. Ran chromatography test: malolactic fermentation is complete. Pressed lightly and sulfited — $1/4$ tsp./ 5 gal. Ended up with 5 gal. + 3 gal. + 3 liters, some of which will be lost as pulp and lees at the next racking. Placed outside to cold stabilize (optional with red wines) and clear. The wine is bitter and tannic again, but has an immense amount of fruit. In hindsight, I should have racked on Day 16, as it was sweeter then, but an extra 4 days on the skins will not make much difference.

5 WEEKS. Wine has good color and clarity. Tastes tannic. pH = 3.65.

9 WEEKS. First racking. Although none of the stoppers had popped, there was a mild hydrogen sulfide odor. So I aerated during racking by trickling the wine down the side of the carboy and added .1 part per million copper sulfate (.15 ml/gal. of 1% $CuSO_4 \cdot 5H_2O$). Some of the H_2S might have converted to mercaptans, but not to disulfides, given the short time on the lees and faintness of the odor. Although there should not be a problem with this wine, this is a good example of the importance of monitoring a wine during the days and weeks immediately after fermentation ceases. The more pulp and sediment, the greater the risk of

problems. Had I left it unattended for a few more weeks, the H_2S would have been converted to mercaptans and possibly disulfides. Have 5 gal. + 2.8 gal. + 1.5 liters. TA tests .73.

16 WEEKS. TA tests .735% and will have to be lowered chemically. Have 5 gal. + 3 gal. The small carboy is earmarked for blending with next fall's Merlot, and will not be adjusted now. Racked 5 gal., adding 12.5 g. calcium carbonate (to lower TA by .1%). No sulfite. May have to add a bit more at the next racking.

17 WEEKS. TA = .62%. Has good flavor, but not much bouquet.

18 WEEKS. TA = .69%. pH = 3.88 — the carbonate raised the pH far more than I wanted or expected. Since the pH is already higher than I would like, I will live with high total acidity. It does not taste acidic.

5 MONTHS. Racked, added 2 cups American oak chips to 5 gal. carboy and 50 ppm sulfite.

8 MONTHS. Racked both carboys.

10 MONTHS. Bottled 5-gal. carboy. Due to the high pH, I added 75 ppm of sulfite at bottling. Holding 3-gal. for blending.

CHARDONNAY

COLD FERMENTATION
Malolactic Fermentation

210 pounds of Chardonnay, 21.5° B at pressing, acid and pH not tested. Grapes had some bunch rot from recent rains, which I sorted/cut out with as much patience as I could muster. Grapes taste sweet but not much flavor. With sugar at this relatively low level, the acid level will be high, and malolactic fermentation looks like a good way to lower it.

DAY 1. Crushed, dissolved and added $\frac{1}{4}$ tsp sulfite per 5 gal of volume. Covered with plastic wrap and soaked on skins for 24 hours to pick up additional flavor.

DAY 2. Pressed, giving the must another half dose of meta (1/8 tsp./5 gal.). Sugar dropped to 21° B after pressing (because pressed juice is slightly lower in sugar than the free-run juice tested yesterday). Inoculated with Montrachet yeast starter. Must has peculiar odor.

DAY 4. Still no sign of fermentation (wine has been in cold garage). Added some yeast lees which was siphoned from a different batch of wine containing Steinberg yeast. Steinberg is active at lower temperatures.

DAY 5. Fermentation under way. Could be either Montrachet or Steinberg — it's probably Steinberg, but it doesn't matter.

DAY 6. Fermentation very active. Transferred to carboys, $3/4$ full; topped with air lock.

DAY 13. Fermenting slowly.

4 WEEKS. Fermenting slowly.

5 WEEKS. Fermenting slowly; still tastes fairly sweet. Combined carboys. Note that with Steinberg yeast it would take several weeks for the last 1% of the sugar to ferment. So I brought it to room temperature to ferment it to total dryness faster. Fermentation picked up as soon as the temperature started to rise.

6 WEEKS. Being held at approx. 70° F (21° C). Fermenting very slowly.

7 WEEKS. One carboy is still, the other ferments slowly.

8 WEEKS. Both carboys are still. Raised ambient temperature to 75-80° F (24-27° C). The next day I stirred in 1 tsp. yeast extract per carboy and malolactic starter (Chr. Hansen *Viniflora Oenos*). Stirred up lees and replaced air lock. The wine will be maintained at 75-80° F (24-27° C) and the nutrients stirred up with a slender dowel until malolactic fermentation is complete. MLF will lower total acid, and the diacetyl produced as a by-product of MLF will give the wine a distinctive "buttery" quality. Stirred twice the next day. It was apparent in two days that MLF had started — carbonization was evident when the lees were stirred up.

9 WEEKS. Effervescence has been slowing of late. Now very little when I stir the lees.

10 WEEKS. No more effervescence. MLF complete-? TA = .73%, which is higher than I would expect after complete MLF. Moved to the garage to cold stabilize and start clarification. Wine tastes very dry, lacks fruit. Needs some character!

11 WEEKS. Chromatography test shows that MLF was just underway when it stopped. The temperature must have dropped lower than I realized (the carboys were sitting directly on the floor). Put the carboys back into the heated area, set on wood blocks to keep it off the floor. Raised ambient temperature to 80° and MLF restarted right away.

12 WEEKS. I stir the lees two or three times a week. The effervescence is a good sign of MLF.

14 WEEKS. Effervescence has slowed noticeably.

15 WEEKS. MLF complete. Set in a cool place to allow the gross lees to settle. Tastes thin, no fruit, does not seem to have much promise.

16 WEEKS. TA = .69%. Has some Chardonnay character.

17 WEEKS. TA = .675% and .69%. pH = 3.39. RS is well under .05%. Tastes even better, like it has some potential! First racking — sulfited (¼ tsp/7 gal), added 8.75 g of calcium carbonate to lower TA by about .05%, and fined with Sparkolloid (1 tsp/gal). Brought inside so it will warm and clear faster.

19 WEEKS. Wine appears clear, but still contains residual haze from Sparkolloid. Stuffed 2 cups of French oak splinters into one carboy, none in the other carboy.

6 MONTHS. Racked, adding 1.8 oz of table sugar to the carboy with oak (to raise TA to about .2%), ⅛ tsp sulfite and fined with 2 oz of liquid beermaker's isinglass per carboy. The carboy without oak received 1.2 oz of sugar for a different style.

8 MONTHS. Bottled with no further racking, even though there was visible haze. The necessary sulfite was added by rinsing the bottles with an intense sulfite solution, draining thoroughly and then adding 1 ml of pre-mixed sulfite solution (¼ tsp sulfite per 25 ml water). The wine does not seem to have much fruit at this stage, but probably will be very good in a couple of years.

FROZEN MUST

CABERNET SAUVIGNON
MALOLACTIC FERMENTATION
Extended Maceration

DAY 1. Picked up 5 gal. frozen must, Sonoma Mountain Cabernet Sauvignon, with skins. Label: 26.5° B sugar; .64 total acid; pH 3.45.

DAY 2. Opened pail—mostly thawed. Dissolved and added ¼ tsp sulfite.

DAY 3. Completely thawed; almost to room temperature. Stirred thoroughly. My readings: 22° B sugar; approx. .9% total acid. (The variance from the label results because one bucket of grapes could have come from any corner of the vineyard and not reflect the average). The must has a great deal of flavor. Added 1 tsp diammonium phosphate and pectic enzyme. Hydrated 1 pkg. Pasteur Red yeast in $\frac{1}{2}$ cup warm water and sprinkled over surface.

DAY 4. Definitely starting to ferment — cap forming. Dumped from pail into 10 gal. primary fermenter and covered. Wine temperature is 67° F (19° C). Took to small heated room which will be heated to approx. 75° F (24° C) for a few days, so the wine will ferment at 80-90° F (27-32° C). Cap will be punched down twice daily from now on.

DAY 5. Fermenting vigorously. Wine temperature is 93° F (34° C), so lowered the room temperature. Added 1 tsp yeast extract and malolactic starter.

DAY 8. Almost still. Wine temperature just under 80° F (27° C). Wine should be tasted daily from now on to see when it mellows.

DAY 12. Very slight cap. RS over 1%, per Clinitest. Chromatography test shows ML is complete. Lowered room temperature to 70° F (21° C).

DAY 14. RS less than .5%. Seems to be still. Tastes more mellow —perhaps.

DAY 15. Tastes harsher - ? If this was the awaited mellowing, it was not very pronounced. Pressed out of concern about the mild hydrogen sulfide odor that has been present for the past several days. This was resulting from autolysis; i.e., active yeast cells consuming other yeast cells. (If the odor had been caused by excess sulfur on the grapes, there would have been an unmistakable rotten egg stink). To be on the safe side, I added .1 ppm of copper (.15 ml per gal. of 1% $CuSO_4 \bullet 5H_2O$). Ended up with 3 gal. + 750 ml + 375 ml. Set outside to cold stabilize and let gross lees settle.

4 WEEKS. First racking. There was so much pulp and lees that I got less than 2.8 gals. of wine from an original 5 gallons, which included skins. Very dark color.

7 WEEKS. Tests .72 TA; .2% RS; pH 3.55. It tastes acidic; the acid will probably need to be lowered.

11 WEEKS. TA tests .73%. TA must be lowered since it still tastes acidic. TA can be lowered chemically using potassium carbonate or with greater accuracy using calcium carbonate. Since the wine will not be bottled for several months, the calcium carbonate will have plenty of time to settle out. I would like to end up with TA just under .6%, but will err on the cautious side initially by adding only enough to lower it by .1% (2.5 X 2.8 gal = 7 g). Dissolved the

calcium carbonate in $^1/_2$ cup of water and added while racking. Set in the corner of a closet until the next racking — calcium carbonate will not precipitate at cold temperatures.

12 WEEKS. TA = .645%. Has nice bouquet, but not much flavor.

13 WEEKS. TA = .67% pH = 3.80. Would like to lower the TA a bit more but will not tinker with it, since the pH is already higher than I would like. It does not taste acidic.

6 MONTHS. Racked.

9 MONTHS. Bottled. Due to the high pH, I used 75 ppm of sulfite at bottling.

2 YEARS. Excellent wine. Took third in a tasting, beating some very pricey California wines!

Lowering pH before fermentation

This is how I handled a different vintage of frozen must, where the pH was high:

Two pails of Sonoma Mountain Cabernet Sauvignon grapes arrive partially thawed. Brix and pH are high, and total acid is low. I plan to lower the pH to approximately 3.50 by adding tartaric acid, regardless of how much it takes or how much it raises total acid. I will lower total acid chemically after fermentation if necessary to get it into the .55–.65% range. Right now, before fermentation, my concern is the high pH—I have to correct it now because I might not be able fully correct it after fermentation.

After the grapes are fully thawed, I blend the 2 pails and mix thoroughly. Dipped out 1 gallon and added 1 tsp. of tartaric acid. This lowered the pH to 3.70. Added another $1/2$ tsp. of tartaric, which lowered pH to 3.60. Added another $1/4$ tsp., which lowered it to 3.50. Based on this result, I know that each additional gallon also needs 1.75 tsp of tartaric to lower the pH to 3.50. Pre-fermentation adjustments are always a little inexact due to the skins, stems, seeds, etc. but at least it's in the right ballpark. The acid tested .85%, which is fine because I plan to put it through malolactic fermentation, which will lower total acid. Acid will drop a little during fermentation and cold stabilization. I will lower it with carbonate later if necessary. The carbonate will raise the pH, but not by much.

RASPBERRY LIQUEUR

Raspberry liqueur is the only fruit wine I continue to make. It is so good that I want to pass along my recipe for the "essence of raspberry," as I call it. If you like port wines or dessert wines, such as Sauternes, ice wines, late harvests, or sweet muscats, this should appeal to you.

If you reveal the recipe first, your friends are guaranteed to snicker—but not after they taste it! The secret is bananas. A pure raspberry liqueur without bananas would be one dimensional and unexceptional. The bananas broaden the raspberry flavor and round out the overall impression of the wine. The more bananas, the mellower the wine will be. Although the ratio of bananas to berries will have an effect on the flavor, the ratio is not critical to success. The following is only a suggestion to be followed on your first attempt. If you want a slightly different result the next time, change the recipe accordingly.

The goal is not to dilute the raspberry flavor and bouquet any more than necessary during the course of fermenting the alcohol level (up to approximately 16%). Always try to minimize the amount of water added; try to get by with the liquid from the sugar syrup, the yeast starter and later from spiking it with Everclear or brandy. You don't get very much wine, but the flavor is intense.

Here are the ingredients which will be needed initially:

1 flat fresh raspberries — approx. 12 lb.

5-7 lb. <u>ripe</u> bananas.

3 lb. raisins.

Pectic enzyme and potassium metabisulfite.

Sugar syrup.

Tokay yeast, which will ferment to a higher alcohol level than most other wine yeasts. Prise de Mousse would also be a good choice.

1 cup "Everclear" (190 proof ethanol) per gallon of finished wine or 2 cups of brandy.

Mash the raspberries in a small primary fermenter and add the raisins. Slice up the bananas and add them. Raspberries have wonderful flavor and bouquet, but contain little sugar and little liquid. The raisins will be a source of sugar as they break down, but more sugar and a little more liquid will be needed. Make a very heavy sugar syrup by dissolving 4 pounds of cane or beet sugar in 2 quarts of boiling water. Add enough of it to the mashed fruit mixture to raise the Brix of the must to approximately 35-40° B. The heat will help rehydrate the raisins and also help break down the berries. If the Brix is much above 40° after the mixture cools, add a little water to lower it. Store the extra syrup in the refrigerator for use later in fermenting or sweetening. After the mixture has cooled, add $1/8$ tsp of meta plus pectic enzyme.

Activate the yeast as described in chapter 2 and inoculate the must when active. The cap should be punched down two or three times a day, as though red grapes were being fermented. This will extract more flavor out of the berries as well as frustrating the aerobic bacteria which might otherwise get established on top of the cap.

Check the remaining unfermented sugar with your hydrometer, and when it drops to 5° B, add more sugar syrup sufficient to raise it to 10-15° B. Try not to exceed 15° B because that seems to be the maximum desired sweetness in a fortified wine and very little of the additional sugar will ferment anyway due to the high alcohol-sugar level.

When fermentation slows to the point where little CO_2 is being produced, pour the entire contents of the pail into a nylon mesh bag and press it by hand (using rubber gloves, of course). Then pour it into a small carboy or gallon jugs to finish fermenting. The jugs should be as full as possible. If you need to fill some air space, add more sliced bananas! Top with an air lock.

When fermentation has slowed to a trickle, it is time to fortify. You want to end up with a liqueur having an alcohol level of approximately 20%. At that level of alcohol, it will be stable and immune to air. This will require about 1 cup of Everclear or 2 cups of brandy per U.S. gallon. You also need to take the volume of pulp into account when spiking. If a fourth of the wine is pulp and solids, reduce the amount of alcohol to be added by one eighth. The solids will not absorb the alcohol, and you don't want the final product to be overly alcoholic.

You can leave it in the jugs to settle. The extensive volume of pulp will compact in a few weeks, and the liqueur will be clear and ready to bottle. This liqueur has a very intense bouquet, so I usually bottle in tenths rather than fifths, or even smaller bottles. The quantity is limited, but the flavor is so intense that small bottles work well.

As mentioned, the final product can be altered by changing the ratio of the ingredients. My first effort consisted of equal amounts of berries, bananas and grapes. I added a small amount of water and sugar syrup as needed and spiked it. The resulting flavor was less concentrated than the above recipe, but I had more wine. It was indistinguishable from a high quality California port. Lower the ratio of bananas to berries and minimize the volume of water going in, and you get a more intense raspberry bouquet and flavor.

Blackberries could be used, but red raspberries are better. Black raspberries should also be good.

SUPPLY SOURCES

FROZEN MUSTS

Peter Brehm has been crushing, pressing and freezing grape musts from Washington and California for many years. Local home winemakers arrange to pick up their fresh grapes or frozen musts at the site; distant winemakers can have frozen musts shipped by UPS. He also sells through a few wine supply shops around the country that have freezer facilities and keep some in stock. It is an expensive proposition, but Brehm goes out of his way to deliver quality. It is a good way to get blending varieties, such as Cabernet Franc, Grenache and Syrah. His website also has a chat board where winemakers can get answers to their fermentation questions.

BREHM VINEYARDS
932 Evelyn Avenue
Albany, CA 94706
Phone: 510-527-3675
FAX: 510-526-1372
E-mail: grapes@BrehmVineyards.com
Website: www.brehmvineyards.com

EQUIPMENT AND SUPPLIES

PRESQUE ISLE WINE CELLARS
9440 W. Main Road
North East, PA 16428
814-728-1314 (information)
800-488-7492 (orders)
FAX 814-725-2092
e-mail: info@piwine.com
website: www.piwine.com

Supplier of grapes, must, fermenting equipment and supplies, plus basic lab glassware and chemicals. Services small wineries as well as home winemakers. Breaks down some Scott color enzymes and lysozyme into practical quantities for home winemakers.

THE WINE LAB
110 Camino Oruga
Napa, CA 94558
707-224-7903
800-224-9463
FAX 707-255-2019
e-mail: winelab@aol.com
website: www.thewinelab.com

Supplier of fermenting equipment and supplies, plus basic lab glassware and chemicals. Services small wineries as well as home winemakers. Has a good malolactic nutrient (Leucofood®). In-depth analyses of musts and wines.

SPAGNOL'S WINE & BEER MAKING SUPPLIES
1325 Derwent Way
Delta, BC
Canada V3M 5V9
800-663-6954
FAX 800-557-7557
website: www.spagnols.com

Supplier in Western Canada of wine grapes, must, concentrates, fermenting supplies and equipment.

NAPA FERMENTATION SUPPLIES
P.O. Box 5839
575 Third Street - Bldg. A
Napa, CA 94581
707-255-6372
FAX 707 255 6462

Supplier of fermenting equipment and supplies for small wineries and home winemakers. Carries imported presses and crusher-stemmers. Also carries basic lab glassware and chemicals.

VINQUIRY
7795 Bell Road
Windsor, CA 95492
Ph. 707-838-6312
FAX 707-838-1765
e-mail: vinquiry@aol.com

Labware, chemicals, reagents and equipment for wineries and advanced home winemakers. Enoferm yeast line. Analytical testing of wines and musts.

ALL WORLD SCIENTIFIC
5515-186th Place S.S.
Lynnwood, WA 98037
Ph. 800-289-6753
FAX 425-776-1530
website: www.awscientific.com

Labware, chemicals, reagents and test equipment for advanced home winemakers.

AMORIM CORK AMERICA
2557 Napa Valley Corporate Dr. #A
Napa, CA 94558
Ph. 707-224-6000
FAX 707-224-7616
website: www.amorimcork.com

OAK SUPPLIES

STAVIN INCORPORATED
P.O. Box 1693
Sausalito, CA 94966
415-331-7849
website: www.stavin.com

Excellent quality oak beans, staves, stave segments, sleeves and infusion tubes for barrels. Available in American, French and European (Hungarian) oaks - medium, medium + and heavy toasts. Sell 228 liter barrels, but nothing smaller.

DEMPTOS NAPA COOPERAGE
1050 Socal Ferry Road
Napa, CA 94558
707-257-2628

Make $7\,^1/_2$, 15 and 30 gal. barrels, French medium toast only (except heads are not toasted). Also sell American oak chips, no staves.

FRANCOIS FRERES D'OREGON
2760 S.E. St. Joseph Rd.
McMinnville, OR 97128
503-472-8883

Make 15 and 30 gal. barrels - French or American oak. Make Oregon oak barrels but only in 228 liter size. Sell Oregon oak chips in small and normal sizes, all 3 toasts.

SEGUIN MOREAU USA
151 Camino Dorado
Napa, CA 94558
707-252-3408

Make 15 and 30 gal. barrels. French oak only - medium toast.

BARREL BUILDERS
1194 Maple Lane
Calistoga, CA 94515
707-942-4291

Brokers Hungarian barrels and represents French cooperage cos.;
makes some handmade barrels. Inventories used barrels.

WORLD COOPERAGE
Phone: (707) 255-5900
Website: www.cooperage.com

Has an extensive line of competitively-priced American oak products as well as foreign.

INNERSTAVE
24200 Arnold Drive
Sonoma, CA 95476
707-996-8781

Good quality oak. French and American oak chips in medium and
medium + toast. Chain-O-Oak for use in barrels or, if split, in carboys - in either French or American oak. No barrels. The company
believes its oak rounds out the mid-palate exceptionally well.

TABLE OF EQUIVALENTS

1 oz.=28.4 g	1 g. = .0353 oz
1 lb.=454 g	1 kg. =2.20 1b
1 fl. oz. =29.6 ml	1 gal. = 128 oz.=3.785 L
1 qt.=.95 L	1 Hecto liter (100 L) =
	26.4 U.S. gallons

One part per million is either 1 gram per million milliliters or 1 milliliter per million milliliters. If you seek a particular level of an active chemical, such as potassium metabisulfite, you have to adjust. In the case of meta, for example, only half the weight becomes free SO_2. So you have to add twice as much to reach the desired level.

1 part per million = .001 g/L = .019 g/5 gal.

1 part per million = 1 ml/264 gal.

TO RAISE TOTAL ACID BY .1%

tartaric acid — add 3.8 g/gal.

malic acid — add 3.4 g/gal.

TO LOWER TOTAL ACID BY .1%

calcium carbonate — add 2.5 g/gal.

potassium carbonate — add 3.8 g/gal.

potassium bicarbonate — add 3.4 g/ gal.

BRIX TO SPECIFIC GRAVITY

Brix	Specific Gravity	Brix	Specific Gravity	Brix	Specific Gravity
0	1.000	9	1.035	18	1.070
1	1.004	10	1.039	19	1.074
2	1.008	11	1.043	20	1.078
3	1.012	12	1.047	21	1.181
4	1.016	13	1.050	22	1.085
5	1.019	14	1.054	23	1.089
6	1.023	15	1.058	24	1.093
7	1.027	16	1.062	25	1.097
8	1.031	17	1.066	26	1.101

Volume-to-Weight Table

Here is a summary of the weight-per-teaspoon of the most common chemicals used by winemakers. Please bear in mind that these are necessarily approximate because some absorb moisture out of the air and some samples will be more compacted than others. As a result, a teaspoon from one source will not weigh the same as a teaspoon from another source. In addition, there can be a sizeable difference from one "teaspoon" to the next. Some spoons vary considerably from 5.0 ml. A scale would obviously be better, but you can get by using these equivalents.

ADDITIVE	GRAMS/TEASPOON
Potassium metabisulfite	5.5-6.3
Tartaric acid	4.7-5.5
Malic acid	4.0-4.6
Gelatin	3.0-3.4
Potassium carbonate	5.7-6.1
Potassium bicarbonate	3.2-3.6
Calcium carbonate	2.4-2.8

SULFITE MANAGEMENT

You need to use potassium metabisulfate if you aspire to making world class wines. Although the dosages recommended earlier in this book are fine for wines with a normal pH, the optimum amount of sulfite varies with the pH of the wine. Those who use barrels will be particularly interested in sulfite management because the level of free sulfite drops about twice as fast in barrels as carboys, and a certain minimum level is needed to protect both the wine and the barrel itself from contamination.

Molecular sulfite

Sulfite binds with acetaldehyde, yeast, bacteria, sugars, and oxygen, but has a higher affinity for some of these constituents than others. It binds most irreversibly with acetaldehyde and proteins, and less so with sugars. Some of the esoteric forms of sugar will eventually release SO_2 that was initially bound. The sulfite that is not bound is known as "free" sulfite. "Total sulfite" is the sum of the bound and free portions, all being expressed either as parts per million or as milligrams per liter. As you will note at the top of the chart on the next page, a miniscule portion of free sulfite consists of "molecular" sulfite. The portion may be tiny, but molecular sulfite is actually the most significant component because it is molecular sulfite that delivers the preservative effect attributed to sulfite in general. Molecular sulfite has a very high affinity for oxygen and reacts immediately with it.

The goal in sulfite management is to maintain just enough free sulfite to get the preservative benefits of some molecular sulfite, but not so much that its negative attributes come forward (namely, the odor). The maximum preservative effect is attained at 2 ppm molecular, but at that level the sulfite odor is objectionable. Balancing odor against preservative benefits, the optimum level is generally regarded as 0.8 ppm molecular. At that level you get adequate antioxidative benefits without suffering an unacceptable odor. Since they contain significant amounts of tannin, a little less sulfite is needed in dry red table wines, with 0.5 ppm molecular generally being regarded as sufficient.

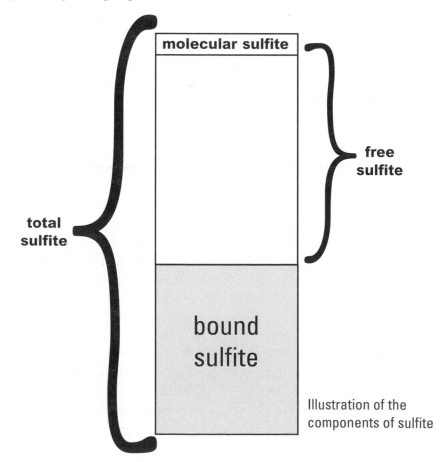

Illustration of the components of sulfite

Molecular sulfite cannot be measured by conventional means, but there is a direct relationship between pH, free sulfite, and molecular sulfite which allows us to derive the molecular amount. If the pH and free sulfite levels are known, the parts per million of molecular sulfite can be determined. This graph shows **the level of free SO₂ required to maintain 0.8 ppm and 0.5 ppm of molecular sulfite at differing pH levels**:

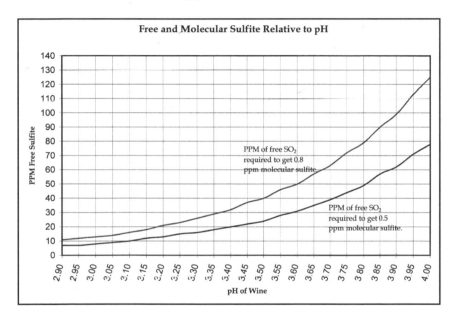

It is at once obvious that the higher the pH, the more free sulfite is needed to get the requisite level of molecular sulfite. At pH 3.6, for example, 50 ppm of free sulfite is needed to maintain 0.8 ppm molecular, whereas only half as much free sulfite is needed at pH 3.3. That is the main reason that wines with pH 3.6 and higher are such a problem — you cannot use enough sulfite in a high pH wine to get the necessary preservative effect without suffering an offensive sulfite odor.

Determining the amount needed

It is assumed that you have the ability to measure both the level of free SO₂ and the pH. The pH is measured with a pH meter, of course. Pocket-sized digital pH meters are available at very reasonable prices these days (see *appendix A*). Free SO₂ is measured by the Ripper method (including Titrets) or preferably by vacuum aspiration, both of which are explained in *appendix A*. As an example of how you work the numbers backward, assume that you have a barrel or carboy of white wine which measures pH 3.4. After several months of aging, a vacuum aspiration test indicates that free SO_2 has dropped to 10 ppm. From the above graph for 0.8 ppm, you know that the desired level of free SO_2 at pH 3.4 is 32 ppm — this is the approximate level that will deliver the optimum 0.8 ppm of molecular sulfite. An additional 22 ppm is needed to get it back up to 32 ppm.

The basic formula to calculate the amount of potassium metabisulfite needed is:

$$\frac{\text{ppm needed x liters of wine}}{0.57}$$

The divisor of 0.57 is needed because only 57% by weight of this compound is the active ingredient, free SO_2. In the above example, if you had a 228-liter barrel of wine, the grams needed would be calculated as follows:

$$\frac{.022 \times 228}{0.57} = 8.8 \text{ g}$$

Adding 8.8 grams of potassium metabisulfite to the barrel will raise the free sulfite by approximately 22 parts per million. This addition, plus the existing 10 ppm already in the wine, will bring free sulfite up to the 32 ppm which the chart indicates is necessary to result in 0.8 ppm of molecular sulfite. If you are using Oensteryl tablets, be aware that "5 grams" on the package means 5 grams of total sulfite; divide by 0.57 to determine the total amount.

Note that when you do the calculations, you cannot just use the raw number "22" in the equation. You have to move the decimal point three places to the left. That's because one part per million is actually 0.001 grams per liter, and twenty-two parts per million is 0.022 grams per liter. This is important because if you are off by only one decimal point, you will get ten times too much SO_2, or one-tenth, either of which could be a disaster.

If you are working with 5 U.S. gallons, you have to first convert the gallons into liters. One gallon is 3.785 liters. Five gallons is 19 liters: $(5 \times 3.785 = 19)$

$$\frac{0.022 \times 19}{0.57} = .73 \text{ g}$$

What if free sulfite does not measure 32 ppm after the addition? This will happen because there is one more variable that enters in. One never knows, until after the fact, exactly how much of a sulfite addition will become bound with aldehydes, sugar, yeast, etc., and how much will remain free. A significant, but unknown amount of sulfite is needed to bind with the aldehydes, proteins and sugar, and only after those needs have been satisfied will the extent of unbound or free sulfite be known. Fortunately, this variable diminishes as the wine ages. At crushing, almost all of a sulfite addition will bind with the sugar and none will remain free at the end of fermentation. At first racking about forty to sixty per cent of an addition will become bound; the rest, by definition, being free sulfite. The percentage becoming bound will go down further with later additions because the wine will have fewer proteins and solids. And much of the remaining solids will already be bound with sulfite from the previous addition, so the wine will have considerably less capacity to absorb another addition. Almost all of it will be free. As a result of this residual nature of free sulfite, it is good practice to run another vacuum aspiration test three or four days after the addition. If it is close to 32 ppm, leave well enough alone. Otherwise, add a little more.

10% stock sulfite solution

Rather than using the above formula to calculate the grams needed and then weighing it and dissolving it in water, it is easier to prepare a 10% stock solution ahead of time. A pre-mixed solution is easier to work with and less prone to error. A 500 ml, brown glass bottle with screw cap works well. Fill the bottle half full of warm water and add 50 grams of potassium metabisulfite (8 tsp.). Shake it until the crystals are dissolved and then top up to 500 ml with cold water. A 750 ml brown wine bottle also works well if the sulfite quantity is also increased by 50%. This stock solution will stay fresh for two months and then should be replaced.

Following (page 220) is a guide as to the volumes of stock solution required for various sulfite levels and volume measurements:

Milliliters of 10% sulfite solution required per:	PARTS PER MILLION OF FREE SO₂ DESIRED		
	10 ppm	30 ppm	50 ppm
Per liter	.18 ml	.53 ml	.88 ml
Per U.S. gal.	.67 ml	2.00 ml	3.33 ml
Per Imp. gal.	.80 ml	2.40 ml	4.00 ml

EXAMPLE 1. If you had just crushed grapes, had 20 gallons U.S. and wanted to add 50 ppm, multiply 20 X 3.32 = 66.4 ml of the 10% stock solution.

EXAMPLE 2. In the pH example above, where you had only 10 ppm, but wanted 32 ppm of free sulfite, you have to add 22 ppm. For a 225-liter barrel, you would add 87.5 ml, calculated as follows: .53 X [22/30] X 225 = 87.5 ml.

Whether you are dissolving it each time or are using a 10% stock solution, you have to stir the must or wine thoroughly to disperse it. This is particularly the case with a must containing skins and pulps. The sulfite will not mix without considerable stirring.

J. Laffort sells a new product known as Oenosteryl which are sulfite tablets that can be dropped into a barrel to boost the level of sulfite. They generate a fizz to help disperse the sulfite, and one tablet delivers sulfite as follows:

Tablet Size	PER U.S. GALLON		PER 5 U.S. GALS.		PER 228 LITERS	
	Total	Free	Total	Free	Total	Free
2-gram	500	300	100	60	9	5
5-gram	1300	750	250	140	22	12

These tablets are a very convenient way to add sulfite without having to rack or stir. If you only need half a dose, split one with a knife and wrap the remainder in foil for future use.

Websites of Interest

http://www.americanwinesociety.com/	American Wine Society
http://wineserver.ucdavis.edu/	University of California at Davis
http://www.makewine.com	Amateur Winemakers of Ontario
http://www.vawa.net	Vancouver Amateur Winemakers Assn
http://www.lafn.org/community/cellarmasters	Cellarmasters
http://www.tomatoweb.com/shw	Sacramento Home Winemakers
http://www.hr/wine/link/	World Wine List
http://www.vine2wine.com	Vine 2 Wine
http://www.geocities.com/NapaValley/1172	Jack Keller's website
http://www.geocities.com/NapaValley/3528	Boeing Employees Beer and Wine Makers Club
http://www.scottlab.com/	Scott Laboratories
http://www.dsm.nl	Gist-brocades yeast
http://www.lallemand.com/	Lalvin Yeasts
http://www.wyeastlab.com/	Wyeast Labs

What's New

Better-Bottle ™ is marketing an extremely light weight plastic carboy which is unbreakable and impermeable to air. A 5-gallon carboy weighs only 18 ounces! The silicone-ringed stoppers and snap-on fittings shown here do not leak and make it easy to rack by gravity. The spigot can be turned to avoid racking lees. The products should be available in beer and winemaking supply shops for the Fall of 2003. The company is experimenting with a variation of the plastic material that would allow minute amounts of oxygen to permeate, which will appeal to red winemakers wanting the benefits of micro-oxidation but not wanting to use barrels,. Website: http://www.better-bottle.com

Index